Love in a Wood by William Wycherley

or, St James Park

*As long as men are false and women vain,
Whilst gold continues to be virtue's bane,
In pointed satire WYCHERLEY shall reign.*
EVELYN.

William Wycherley was born at Clive near Shrewsbury, Shropshire and baptised on April 8th, 1641 at Whitchurch in Hampshire where it is thought he spent some time before his family settled in Malappuram, India.

At the age of he was sent to France to be educated in France. It was here that he converted to Roman Catholicism. Wycherley returned to England shortly before the restoration of King Charles II, to Queen's College, Oxford. Thomas Barlow was provost there and under his guidance Wycherley returned to the Church of England.

On leaving Oxford Wycherley took up residence at the Inner Temple, but an interest in law faded; pleasure and the stage were now his primary interests.

His play, Love in a Wood, was produced early in 1671 at the Theatre Royal, Drury Lane. It was daring and he became the talk of the Court. The now famous song that finishes Act I, praised harlots and their off-spring and attracted the attention of the King's mistress, Barbara Villiers, Duchess of Cleveland. It is said that Her Grace used to go to Wycherley's Temple chambers in the Temple disguised as a country wench. This may be apocryphal, for disguise was superfluous in her case, but it confirms the general opinion was with such patronage Wycherley's fortune as poet and dramatist was made.

Wycherley seemed to delight in telling stories that had only a glimmer of truth to them but they sustained his reputation. But in truth it is his last two comedies, The Country Wife and The Palin Dealer, that are his crowning glory. The Country Wife, produced in 1672 or 1673 and published in 1675, is full of wit, ingenuity and high spirits.

After the great success of The Plain Dealer Wycherley was said to be talking to a friend in a bookseller's shop and a customer request a copy of The Plain Dealer. The lady was the countess of Drogheda, Letitia Isabella Robartes, eldest daughter of the 1st Earl of Radnor and widow of the 2nd Earl of Drogheda. An introduction was secured and soon marriage. Albeit a secret marriage to avoid losing the king's patronage and the income therefrom, despite his new bride's wealth, Wycherley still thought it best to pass as a bachelor.

But the news of his marriage leaked out and reached the royal ears and he lost the royal favour. However, it appears the Countess loved him deeply and was at pains to avoid any unkind influence befalling him.

Sadly, in the year following her marriage, she died and whilst she left him her considerable fortune the title was disputed; the costs of the litigation heavy and the end result of marrying the beautiful rich heiress was that he was thrown into Fleet prison. He remained there for seven years, being released only after James II had been so sated by seeing The Plain Dealer that he paid off Wycherley's execution creditor and settled on him a pension of £200 a year.

Other debts still troubled Wycherley, however, and he never was released from his embarrassments, not even after succeeding to a life estate in the family property.

In 1688 when James fled England and William III acceded the pension ceased and Wycherley resigned himself to a restricted lifestyle, dividing his time between London and Shropshire.

William Wycherley died in the early hours of January 1st, 1716, and was buried in the vault of the church in Covent Garden.

Index of Contents
INTRODUCTION
WILLIAM WYCHERLEY
LOVE IN A WOOD; or ST. JAMES'S PARK
TO HER GRACE THE DUCHESS OF CLEVELAND
DRAMATIS PERSONÆ
SCENE:—LONDON
PROLOGUE
LOVE IN A WOOD; or, ST. JAMES'S PARK
ACT THE FIRST
SCENE I.—Gripe's House, in the evening
SCENE II.—The French House
ACT THE SECOND
SCENE I.—St. James's Park at night
SCENE II.—Christina's Lodging
SCENE III.—The Street before Christina's Lodging
SCENE IV.—Vincent's Lodging
ACT THE THIRD
SCENE I.—A Room in Mrs Crossbite's House
SCENE II.—Mrs Crossbite's Dining-room
SCENE III.—A Room in Mrs Crossbite's House
SCENE IV.—Lydia's Lodging
ACT THE FOURTH
SCENE I.—A Room in Gripe's House
SCENE II.—Another Room in the same
SCENE III.—The old Pall Mall
SCENE IV.—The Street before Vincent's Lodging
SCENE V.—Vincent's Lodging
ACT THE FIFTH
SCENE I.—St. James's Park
SCENE II.—Another part of the same
SCENE III.—Another part of the same
SCENE IV.—Another part of the same

SCENE V.—Another part of the same
SCENE VI.—The Dining-room in Mulberry-garden House
EPILOGUE

INTRODUCTION

William Wycherley was, before Congreve arose to surpass him, the most eminent master of that artificial school of Comedy which commenced with the restoration of Charles II., and which may be said to have perished, in a blaze as of a funeral pyre, with Sheridan. Abandoning the beaten paths of English drama, the writers of this school found, in the various intrigue of the Spanish theatre, in the verbal vivacity and piquant satire of the French, a new basis for their productions. Their works, as a class, have been designated the Comedy of Manners, a title which aptly distinguishes them from the Comedy of Human Life, set forth by Shakespeare. It is a title, nevertheless, of limited applicability. The manners portrayed in these comedies, if drawn from the life, illustrate but one side of human character, and that side the most superficial. To divert by wit and ingenuity being the writer's aim, all allusion to the deeper motives of humanity was rejected as impertinent, or admitted only as an occasional contrast to the prevailing tone. Thus the artificiality of the characters is the consequence rather of incompleteness than of untruth; they are, as it were, but half characters; the dialogue is no longer, as with Shakespeare, the means of their development, but the purpose of their creation.

Living in an age of loose manners and corrupt morals, the result, as has often been pointed out, of the unnatural state of repression which accompanied the Puritan supremacy, Wycherley cannot be acquitted of the vices of his time, nor can it be contended that it was altogether with the object of lashing these vices that he decked them out with all the allurements of brilliant dialogue and diverting situations. Yet I venture to assert that, in spite of their licentiousness, these comedies possess claims to recognition not lightly to be ignored. Nay, more: that their very indecency, although the most open, is certainly not the most pernicious form of immorality known to us in literature. For as the harm of licentious allusions consists in their appeal to the basest passions of human nature, so the appeal is stronger as the impression of human passion is deeper. But these simulacra, these puppet semblances of humanity, which Wycherley and his contemporaries summon upon the stage for our diversion, what human passion can we discover in these to which we should be in danger of unworthily responding? As we read the plays no sense of reality disturbs us. Transfer the language they employ, the actions they perform, to the characters in a play of Shakespeare's, a novel of Richardson's, and our resentment and detestation are instantly awakened. But the dramatis personæ of Wycherley or of Congreve are not, as the characters of Shakespeare and Richardson, men and women whom we feel to be as real and living as those with whom we daily associate. They merely simulate humanity so far as is requisite for the proper enactment of their parts. And herein lies the test: a Cordelia, an Iago, a Clarissa, a Lovelace, are, to our feelings, real creatures of flesh and blood, whom we love or hate, as the case may be. The characters of Wycherley and Congreve, on the contrary, we neither love nor detest; we are interested not in what they are, but only in what they say and do. They have no further existence for us than as they act and speak on the stage before our eyes; touch them, and, like ghosts in Elysium, they turn to empty air in our grasp.

Another counter-influence to the unwholesomeness of these comedies is the current of mirth which runs through them, more or less, from end to end. For laughter may be reckoned in some sort an antidote to sensuality, at least to sensuality in its vilest and most insinuating mood. "There is no passion," as Sterne says, "so serious as lust;" and we may safely conclude that when laughter is provoked, the wit of expression or the ludicrousness of situation is more active to our apprehension than the license of sentiment.

It is sometimes urged against the comedies of this school that Virtue, in them, is brought on the stage only to be derided. But this charge is manifestly unjust. Virtue, indeed, is an unfrequent guest in this house of mirth; she finds a refuge in the house of mourning hard by, in the tragedies of the times. Yet if she chance to cross the unwonted threshold, it is not to be laughed out of countenance, but more often to be entertained as an honoured guest. Take, for instance, the character of Christina, in Wycherley's Love in a Wood, or even that of Alithea, in The Country Wife; the sentiments of honour and purity that are set on their lips, or expressed in their actions, are evidently intended to excite our esteem and admiration. Nay, it may even be affirmed that if, among these shadowy creatures, there be any that affect us, beyond the others, with some sense of an approach to living reality, it is precisely the virtuous characters from whom such an impression is derived. It is true, on the other hand, that the sin of adultery, so common to the dramatic plots of this period, is treated not only without severity, but as a pleasant jest. To the husbands, in general, small mercy is shown. Yet what husbands are these—these Pinchwifes, Fondlewifes, et hoc genus omne? It is less the sanctity of marriage that is attacked, or held up to ridicule, in their persons, than their own vices, their jealousy, tyranny, or folly. And, after all, it is by no means in the crime itself, but in the ingenuity of intrigue, that we are expected to find diversion; and the utter absence of genuine passion on the part of these stage criminals renders any appeal to passion in ourselves out of the question.

It is not with any intention of excusing the license which abounds in Wycherley's comedies that I have ventured to offer these few considerations in their behalf. I contend only that their laughing outrages upon decency, are infinitely less harmful, because more superficial, than the sentimental lewdness which, arising from a deeper depravity, instils a more subtle venom; that, condemn it as we needs must, we may yet stop short of attaching to the immorality of the dramatists of the Restoration such consequence as to debar ourselves, for its sake, from enjoying to the full the admirable wit and ingenuity which constitute the chief merit of their performances.

Wycherley produced but four comedies, which, however, contain almost all of intrinsic value that remains from his pen. Besides these, he himself published but one volume, a folio of Miscellany-Poems, which appeared in 1704, when the author was sixty-four years of age. Of these pieces nothing favourable can be affirmed even by the friendliest critic. They form a strange olla podrida of so-called philosophy and obscenity; they are dull without weight, or lewd without wit; or if even here and there a good thought occur, the ore is scarcely of such value as to be worth the pains of separating from the dross. The book suggests a curious picture of the veteran dramatist, ever and anon laying aside his favourite Rochefoucauld or Montaigne to chuckle feebly over the reminiscence of some smutty story of his youthful days. The versification is, as Macaulay says, beneath criticism; Wycherley had no spark of poetry in his whole composition. In fine, we may apply to this volume, without qualification, Dryden's remarks upon poor Elkanah Settle; "His style is boisterous and rough-hewn; his rhyme incorrigibly lewd, and his numbers perpetually harsh and ill-sounding." Yet there is one thing which redeems the volume from utter contempt, as a testimony, not, indeed, to the author's talent, but to the constancy and disinterestedness of his temper. I refer to the brave verses addressed to his friend the Duke of Buckingham, on the occasion of that versatile nobleman's disgrace and imprisonment in the Tower. The key note is struck in the opening lines:

"Your late Disgrace is but the Court's Disgrace,

as its false accusation but your Praise."

These lines, it may be remarked, are intended as a rhymed couplet, and may serve as one instance out of many of the "incorrigible lewdness" of Wycherley's rhyme; but, paltry as the verses may be, the feeling which prompted them was surely deserving of respect.

The pieces in prose and verse, which, "having the misfortune to fall into the hands of a mercenary, were published in 1728, in 8vo, under the title of The Posthumous Works of William Wycherley Esq.," are on the whole superior to the Miscellany-Poems, yet, excepting perhaps some of the prose aphorisms which constitute the first part of the collection, little or nothing is to be found, even here, worth resuscitating. Such facility or occasional elegance as the verses possess must be wholly ascribed to the corrections of Pope; but Pope himself failed in the impracticable attempt to make a silk purse out of a sow's ear. Some few of the best pieces, as the lines on Solitude, might possibly pass muster as the worst in a better volume, while the epistle to Dryden (who had invited Wycherley's collaboration in the construction of a comedy—an honour which the younger author gratefully and modestly declined) is interesting personally, and the strain of elaborate compliment, to which, after the fashion of the day, Wycherley treated his correspondents, is here, for once, not wholly misapplied. The Maxims, however, contain better stuff than the verses, and fully justify Pope's repeated hints to the author that "the greater part" of his pieces "would make a much better figure as single maxims and reflections in prose, after the manner of your favourite Rochefoucauld, than in verse." Although, for the most part, as trite as moral aphorisms usually are, they are not without here and there a touch of wit, of terseness, or even of wisdom. Here, for instance, is a pretty simile:—"False friends, like the shadow upon a dial, are ever present to the sunshine of our fortunes, and as soon gone when we begin to be under a cloud." Here, again, is a touch of characteristic satire:—"Old men give young men good counsel, not being able longer to give them bad examples." And for a specimen of his wisdom take the following:—"The silence of a wise man is more wrong to mankind than the slanderer's speech."

I have now noticed all that has appeared in print of Wycherley's authorship beyond his letters to Pope (which possess at least the merit of occasioning Pope's letters to Wycherley), and a few letters of earlier date, published by Dennis, which contain, however, nothing of more consequence than a string of extravagant and affected encomiums upon his correspondent. Something remains to be said on the subject of our author's personal character, which I shall endeavour to set in a juster light than that in which it is presented by Macaulay, whose vivid scrutiny, like a strong torch-light, brings out the worse parts into sharp relief, while it leaves the better in dense obscurity. It is not to be doubted that Wycherley participated in the fashionable follies and vices of the age in which he lived. His early intrigue with the Duchess of Cleveland was notorious. The license of his own writings is a standing witness against him, and the indecency of some of the verses which he published in his old age proves that his mind reverted to the scenes of his youth with feelings other than those of a repentant sinner. Yet in accepting the evidence of Wycherley's writings we should beware of over-rating its importance. Dryden's character is well known as that of a modest and excellent man; yet Dryden occasionally produced passages abundantly obscene. Libertinism was the fashion of the age, and although the fashion had somewhat changed when Wycherley published his Miscellany-Poems, we can feel little surprise that the productions of an aged and infirm man should be redolent rather of the days when he was crowned with honours and sated with success, than of those later years of ill-health and obscurity. In this man's composition the clay was assuredly mingled with pure metal. Nothing in the testimony of his contemporaries is so striking as the tone of affection and esteem which they continually assume in speaking of him. Dryden writes to John Dennis that he has laid aside his intention of commenting upon some friend's purpose of marriage; "for, having had the Honour to see my Dear Friend Wycherley's

Letter to him on that occasion, I find nothing to be added or amended. But as well as I love Mr. Wycherley, I confess I love myself so well, that I will not shew how much I am inferior to him in Wit and Judgment, by undertaking anything after him." And Dryden's regard was gratefully and cordially reciprocated. In his first letter to Wycherley Pope refers to the high satisfaction which he experienced in hearing the old dramatist, at their very first meeting, "doing justice to his dead friend, Mr. Dryden." Wycherley's own epistle, in verse, to the great poet I have already mentioned; it is filled with expressions, sincere if exaggerated, of regard and admiration; and long after Dryden's death, in an essay which appeared not until its author had, himself, been years in his grave, Wycherley writes of "my once good friend, Mr. Dryden, whose Memory will be honour'd when I have no Remembrance."

His attachment to his friends, indeed, appears to have been a prominent characteristic of his disposition. Major Pack, in a short memoir prefixed to the Posthumous Works, declares that "he was as impatient to hear his Friend calumniated, as some other people would be to find themselves defamed. I have more than once," he adds, "been a witness of that honourable Tenderness in his Temper."

His friendship with Pope is one of the best known incidents in his life. It commenced in 1704, when Wycherley was sixty-four and Pope but sixteen years of age, and, although at times interrupted, terminated only with the death of the former in 1715. Their correspondence displays on both sides the marks of sincere regard. Wycherley's generous appreciation the young genius repaid with gratitude and affection, which, however, in the moments even of its warmest ardour, never degenerated into servility. The last published letter between them is dated May 2, 1710. It was succeeded by a period of prolonged estrangement. During the preceding year a silence of unusual duration on the part of Wycherley had aroused the anxiety of Pope, who alludes to it, in his correspondence with their common friend Cromwell, in terms of heart-felt concern. Wycherley had been dangerously ill, and Cromwell had acquainted Pope with the news of his recovery.

"You have delivered me," he replies, under date of Oct. 19, 1709, "from more anxiety than he imagines me capable of on his account, as I am convinced by his long silence. However the love of some things rewards itself, as of Virtue, and of Mr. Wycherley. I am surprised at the danger you tell me he has been in, and must agree with you that our nation would have lost in him as much wit and probity, as would have remained (for aught I know) in the rest of it. My concern for his friendship will excuse me (since I know you honour him so much, and since you know I love him above all men) if I vent a part of my uneasiness to you, and tell you that there has not been wanting one to insinuate malicious untruths of me to Mr. Wycherley, which, I fear, may have had some effect upon him."

The correspondence was renewed, with all the old kindness, in the following spring, but was soon again to be interrupted. Pope had, for some years, been engaged upon the occasional correction and emendation of Wycherley's worse than mediocre verses, and the unsparing honesty with which he discharged this delicate office, however creditable to his character, could not but be at times unpalatable to the author now seventy years of age, and rendered peevish by ill-health and loss of memory. His last published letter to Pope betrays some natural indignation at the wholesale slaughter which the young poet was making of his halting lines, although, with the politeness of an old courtier, he thanks him for his freedom, which he "shall always acknowledge with all sort of gratitude." It is probable, also, that some enemy of Pope had again possessed the old man's ear with slanders, to which his shattered memory would render him the more accessible, and Wycherley again broke off the correspondence, leaving his friend to wonder how he had displeased him, as knowing himself "guilty of no offence but of doing sincerely just what he bid me."

Pope's references to Wycherley, during this new estrangement, show him to have been deeply hurt. They indicate, however, more of sorrow than of resentment, and his delight was unfeigned when, in the autumn of 1711, his friend was once more reconciled to him, and once more wrote to him and spoke of him in terms of the warmest affection. Cromwell, from whose correspondence with Pope we derive our information regarding this second reconciliation narrates the following pleasant incident.

"Mr. Wycherley came to town on Sunday last, and, kindly surprised me with a visit on Monday morning. We dined and drank together; and I saying, 'To our loves,' he replied, 'It is Mr. Pope's health.'" On these terms we leave them. Their correspondence of this date has not been made public, nor do we know if malice or misunderstanding again destroyed the concord thus happily re-established. Pope's letters to Cromwell, moreover, cease about this time, and those which he addressed to others contain no further mention of Wycherley, until in January 1716, he describes to Mr. Blount the closing scene of the life of "that eminent comic poet, and our friend."

In after years, speaking of Wycherley, Pope said: "We were pretty well together to the last: only his memory was so totally bad, that he did not remember a kindness done to him, even from minute to minute. He was peevish, too, latterly; so that sometimes we were out a little, and sometimes in. He never did an unjust thing to me in his whole life; and I went to see him on his death-bed."

One more of his contemporaries I propose to bring forward as a witness to our author's character. George Granville, Baron Lansdowne, to the ordinary qualifications of an accomplished gentleman added some pretensions, not altogether contemptible, to the rank of a minor poet. He was the author of a vast number of elegantly written verses (usually addressed to "Mira"), of a tragedy (Heroic Love) commended by Dryden, and of an amusing comedy (Once a Lover and always a Lover) of the school of Wycherley and Congreve. In the second volume of his collected works is to be found an epistle in which he remarks, with some minuteness, upon the character and disposition of his friend Wycherley.

This letter is not dated, but, from internal evidence, must have been written about the year 1705 or 1706. Lansdowne sets out with declaring that his partiality to Wycherley as a friend might render what he says of him suspected, "if his Merit was not so well and so publickly established as to set him above Flattery. To do him barely Justice," he continues, "is an Undertaking beyond my Skill." Further he writes: "As pointed and severe as he is in his Writings, in his Temper he has all the Softness of the tenderest Disposition; gentle and inoffensive to every Man in his particular Character; he only attacks Vice as a publick Enemy, compassionating the Wound he is under a Necessity to probe." Yet, "in my Friend every Syllable, every Thought is masculine;" and it was, questionless, from this particularity that he acquired the sobriquet (alluding, at the same time, to The Plain Dealer) of Manly Wycherley. Of our Plain Dealer as a poet Lansdowne candidly confesses—"It is certain he is no Master of Numbers; but a Diamond is not less a Diamond for not being polish'd." And then, addressing his correspondent: "Congreve," he writes, "is your familiar Acquaintance, you may judge of Wycherley by him: they have the same manly way of Thinking and Writing, the same Candour, Modesty, Humanity, and Integrity of Manners: It is impossible not to love them for their own Sakes, abstracted from the Merit of their Works." In conclusion Lansdowne invites his correspondent to his lodging, to meet Wycherley, as well as "a young Poet, newly inspired," whose "Name is Pope," who "is not above seventeen or eighteen years of age, and promises Miracles," and whom Wycherley and Walsh "have taken under their Wing."

The foregoing testimonies are, I venture to think, sufficiently explicit. Johnson, indeed, supposes Wycherley to have been "esteemed without virtue, and caressed without good-humour," but a statement so obviously self-contradictory deserves no consideration. One thing is clear: that Wycherley was both beloved and honoured by men whose temper and capacity give irrefragable authority to their judgment, and that judgment, based, as it was upon personal and intimate acquaintance, it were presumption to dispute.

The present text is that of the first editions, which I have carefully collated with, and occasionally corrected by, the text of the edition of 1713 (the last published during the author's life), and that of Leigh Hunt's edition of 1849. I have usually followed the punctuation of Leigh Hunt, who was the first to punctuate the plays accurately.

WM. C. WARD.

WILLIAM WYCHERLEY

William Wycherley was born in 1640. He was the son of a Shropshire gentleman of old family, and of what was then accounted a good estate. The property was estimated at £600 a year, a fortune which, among the fortunes at that time, probably ranked as a fortune of £2,000 a year would rank in our days.

William was an infant when the civil war broke out; and, while he was still in his rudiments, a Presbyterian hierarchy and a republican government were established on the ruins of the ancient church and throne. Old Mr. Wycherley was attached to the royal cause, and was not disposed to intrust the education of his heir to the solemn Puritans who now ruled the universities and the public schools. Accordingly, the young gentleman was sent at fifteen to France. He resided some time in the neighbourhood of the Duke of Montausier, chief of one of the noblest families of Touraine. The Duke's wife, a daughter of the house of Rambouillet, was a finished specimen of those talents and accomplishments for which her house was celebrated. The young foreigner was introduced to the splendid circle which surrounded the duchess, and there he appears to have learned some good and some evil. In a few years he returned to this country a fine gentleman and a Papist. His conversion, it may safely be affirmed, was the effect not of any strong impression on his understanding or feelings, but partly of intercourse with an agreeable society in which the Church of Rome was the fashion, and partly of that aversion to Calvinistic austerities which was then almost universal amongst young Englishmen of parts and spirit, and which, at one time, seemed likely to make one half of them Catholics and the other half Atheists.

But the Restoration came. The universities were again in loyal hands, and there was reason to hope that there would be again a national church fit for a gentleman. Wycherley became a member of Queen's College, Oxford, and abjured the errors of the Church of Rome. The somewhat equivocal glory of turning, for a short time, a good-for-nothing Papist into a very good-for-nothing Protestant is ascribed to Bishop Barlow.

Wycherley left Oxford without taking a degree, and entered at the Temple, where he lived gaily for some years, observing the humours of the town, enjoying its pleasures and picking up just as much law as was necessary to make the character of a pettifogging attorney or of a litigious client entertaining in a comedy.

From an early age, he had been in the habit of amusing himself by writing. Some wretched lines of his on the Restoration are still extant. Had he devoted himself to the making of verses, he would have been nearly as far below Tate and Blackmore as Tate and Blackmore are below Dryden. His only chance for renown would have been that he might have occupied a niche in a satire between Flecknoe and Settle. There was, however, another kind of composition in which his talents and acquirements qualified him to succeed; and to that he judiciously betook himself.

In his old age he used to say that he wrote Love in a Wood at nineteen, The Gentleman Dancing-Master at twenty-one, the Plain Dealer at twenty-five, and The Country Wife at one or two and thirty. We are incredulous, we own, as to the truth of this story. Nothing that we know of Wycherley leads us to think him incapable of sacrificing truth to vanity. And his memory in the decline of his life played him such strange tricks that we might question the correctness of his assertion without throwing any imputation on his veracity. It is certain that none of his plays was acted till 1672, when he gave Love in a Wood to the public. It seems improbable that he should resolve, on so important an occasion as that of a first appearance before the world, to run his chance with a feeble piece, written before his talents were ripe, before his style was formed, before he had looked abroad into the world; and this when he had actually in his desk two highly finished plays, the fruit of his matured powers. When we look minutely at the pieces themselves, we find in every part of them reason to suspect the accuracy of Wycherley's statement. In the first scene of Love in a Wood, to go no further, we find many passages which he could not have written when he was nineteen. There is an allusion to gentlemen's periwigs, which first came into fashion in 1663; an allusion to guineas, which were first struck in 1663; an allusion to the vests which Charles ordered to be worn at court in 1666; an allusion to the fire of 1666; and several allusions to political and ecclesiastical affairs which must be assigned to times later than the year of the Restoration—to times when the government and the city were opposed to each other, and when the Presbyterian ministers had been driven from the parish churches to the conventicles. But it is needless to dwell on particular expressions. The whole air and spirit of the piece belong to a period subsequent to that mentioned by Wycherley. As to The Plain Dealer, which is said to have been written when he was twenty-five, it contains one scene unquestionably written after 1675, several which are later than 1668, and scarcely a line which can have been composed before the end of 1666.

Whatever may have been the age at which Wycherley composed his plays, it is certain that he did not bring them before the public till he was upwards of thirty. In 1672, Love in a Wood was acted with more success than it deserved, and this event produced a great change in the fortunes of the author. The Duchess of Cleveland cast her eyes upon him and was pleased with his appearance. This abandoned woman, not content with her complaisant husband and her royal keeper, lavished her fondness on a crowd of paramours of all ranks, from dukes to rope-dancers. In the time of the Commonwealth she commenced her career of gallantry, and terminated it under Anne, by marrying, when a great grandmother, that worthless fop, Beau Fielding. It is not strange that she should have regarded Wycherley with favour. His figure was commanding, his countenance strikingly handsome, his look and deportment full of grace and dignity. He had, as Pope said long after, "the true nobleman look," the look which seems to indicate superiority, and a not unbecoming consciousness of superiority. His hair indeed, as he says in one of his poems, was prematurely grey. But in that age of periwigs this misfortune was of little importance.

The Duchess admired him, and proceeded to make love to him after the fashion of the coarse-minded and shameless circle to which she belonged. In the Ring, when the crowd of beauties and fine gentlemen was thickest, she put her head out of her coach-window and bawled to him—"Sir, you are a rascal; you are a villain;" and, if she is not belied, she added another phrase of abuse which we will not quote, but of which we may say that it might most justly have been applied to her own children. Wycherley called on her Grace the next day, and with great humility begged to know in what way he had been so unfortunate as to disoblige her. Thus began an intimacy from which the poet probably expected wealth and honours. Nor were such expectations unreasonable. A handsome young fellow about the court, known by the name of Jack Churchill was, about the same time, so lucky as to become the object of a short-lived fancy of the Duchess. She had presented him with £4,500, the price, in all probability, of some title or some pardon. The prudent youth had lent the money on high interest and on landed security; and this judicious investment was the beginning of the most splendid private fortune in Europe. Wycherley was not so lucky. The partiality with which the great lady regarded him was indeed the talk of the whole town; and, sixty years later, old men who remembered those days told Voltaire that she often stole from the court to her lover's chambers in the Temple, disguised like a country girl, with a straw hat on her head, pattens on her feet and a basket in her hand.

The poet was indeed too happy and proud to be discreet. He dedicated to the Duchess the play which had led to their acquaintance, and in the dedication expressed himself in terms which could not but confirm the reports which had gone abroad. But at Whitehall such an affair was regarded in no serious light. The lady was not afraid to bring Wycherley to court and to introduce him to a splendid society, with which, as far as appears, he had never before mixed. The easy king, who allowed to his mistresses the same liberty which he claimed for himself, was pleased with the conversation and manners of his new rival. So high did Wycherley stand in the royal favour that once, when he was confined by a fever to his lodgings in Bow Street, Charles, who, with all his faults, was certainly a man of social and affable disposition, called on him, sat by his bed, advised him to try a change of air, and gave him a handsome sum of money to defray the expenses of a journey. Buckingham, then Master of the Horse and one of that infamous ministry known by the name of the Cabal, had been one of the Duchess's innumerable paramours. He at first showed some symptoms of jealousy, but he soon, after his fashion, veered round from anger to fondness, and gave Wycherley a commission in his own regiment and a place in the royal household.

It would be unjust to Wycherley's memory not to mention here the only good action, as far as we know, of his whole life. He is said to have made great exertions to obtain the patronage of Buckingham for the illustrious author of Hudibras, who was now sinking into an obscure grave, neglected by a nation proud of his genius and by a court which he had served too well. His grace consented to see poor Butler; and an appointment was made. But unhappily two pretty women passed by; the volatile Duke ran after them; the opportunity was lost and could never be regained.

The second Dutch war, the most disgraceful war in the whole history of England, was now raging. It was not in that age considered as by any means necessary that a naval officer should receive a professional education. Young men of rank, who were hardly able to keep their feet in a breeze, served on board the King's ships, sometimes with commissions and sometimes as volunteers. Mulgrave, Dorset, Rochester, and many others left the playhouses and the Mall for hammocks and salt pork; and, ignorant as they were of the rudiments of naval service, showed, at least, on the day of battle, the courage which is seldom wanting in an English gentleman. All good judges of maritime affairs complained that, under this system, the ships were grossly mismanaged, and that the tarpaulins contracted the vices, without acquiring the graces, of the court. But on this subject, as on every other, the government of Charles was deaf to all remonstrances where the interests or whims of favourites were concerned. Wycherley did not choose to be out of the fashion. He embarked, was present at a battle, and celebrated it, on his return, in a copy of verses too bad for the bellman.

About the same time he brought on the stage his second piece, The Gentleman Dancing-Master. The biographers say nothing, as far as we remember, about the fate of this play. There is, however, reason to believe that, though certainly far superior to Love in a Wood, it was not equally successful. It was first tried at the west end of the town, and, as the poet confessed, "would scarce do there." It was then performed in Salisbury Court, but, as it should seem, with no better event. For, in the prologue to The Country Wife, Wycherley described himself as "the late so baffled scribbler."

In 1675, The Country Wife was performed with brilliant success, which, in a literary point of view, was not wholly unmerited. For, though one of the most profligate and heartless of human compositions, it is the elaborate production of a mind, not indeed rich, original or imaginative, but ingenious, observant, quick to seize hints, and patient of the toil of polishing.

The Plain Dealer, equally immoral and equally well written, appeared in 1677. At first this piece pleased the people less than the critics; but after a time its unquestionable merits and the zealous support of Lord Dorset, whose influence in literary and fashionable society was unbounded, established it in the public favour.

The fortune of Wycherley was now in the zenith and began to decline. A long life was still before him. But it was destined to be filled with nothing but shame and wretchedness, domestic dissensions, literary failures and pecuniary embarrassments.

The King, who was looking about for an accomplished man to conduct the education of his natural son, the young Duke of Richmond, at length fixed on Wycherley. The poet, exulting in his good luck, went down to amuse himself at Tunbridge, looked into a bookseller's shop on the Pantiles, and, to his great delight, heard a handsome woman ask for The Plain Dealer, which had just been published. He made acquaintance with the lady, who proved to be the Countess of Drogheda, a gay young widow with an ample jointure. She was charmed with his person and his wit, and after a short flirtation, agreed to become his wife. Wycherley seems to have been apprehensive that this connection might not suit well with the King's plans respecting the Duke of Richmond. He accordingly prevailed on the lady to consent to a private marriage. All came out. Charles thought the conduct of Wycherley both disrespectful and disingenuous. Other causes probably assisted to alienate the sovereign from the subject who had lately been so highly favoured. Buckingham was now in opposition and had been committed to the Tower; not, as Mr. Leigh Hunt supposes, on a charge of treason, but by an order of the House of Lords for some expressions which he had used in debate. Wycherley wrote some bad lines in praise of his imprisoned patron, which, if they came to the knowledge of the King, would certainly have made his majesty very angry. The favour of the court was completely withdrawn from the poet. An amiable woman with a large fortune might indeed have been an ample compensation for the loss. But Lady Drogheda was ill-tempered, imperious and extravagantly jealous. She had herself been a maid of honour at Whitehall. She well knew in what estimation conjugal fidelity was held among the fine gentlemen there, and watched her town husband as assiduously as Mr. Pinchwife watched his country wife. The unfortunate wit was, indeed, allowed to meet his friends at a tavern opposite to his own house. But on such occasions the windows were always open, in order that her ladyship, who was posted on the other side of the street, might be satisfied that no woman was of the party.

The death of Lady Drogheda released the poet from this distress; but a series of disasters in rapid succession broke down his health, his spirits and his fortune. His wife meant to leave him a good property and left him only a lawsuit. His father could not or would not assist him. He was at length thrown into the Fleet, and languished there during seven years, utterly forgotten, as it should seem, by the gay and lively circle of which he had been a distinguished ornament. In the extremity of his distress, he implored the publisher who had been enriched by the sale of his works to lend him twenty pounds, and was refused. His comedies, however, still kept the stage and drew great audiences, which troubled themselves little about the situation of the author. At length, James the Second, who had now succeeded to the throne, happened to go to the theatre on an evening when The Plain Dealer was acted. He was pleased with the performance, and touched by the fate of the writer, whom he probably remembered as one of the gayest and handsomest of his brother's courtiers. The King determined to pay Wycherley's debts and to settle on the unfortunate poet a pension of £200 a-year. This munificence on the part of a prince who was little in the habit of rewarding literary merit, and whose whole soul was devoted to the interests of his Church, raises in us a surmise which Mr. Leigh Hunt will, we fear, pronounce very uncharitable. We cannot help suspecting that it was at this time that Wycherley returned to the communion of the Church of Rome. That he did return to the communion of the Church of Rome is certain. The date of his reconversion, as far as we know, has never been mentioned by any biographer. We believe that, if we place it at this time, we do no injustice to the character either of Wycherley or James.

Not long after, old Mr. Wycherley died; and his son, now past the middle of life, came to the family estate. Still, however, he was not at his ease. His embarrassments were great; his property was strictly tied up; and he was on very bad terms with the heir-at-law. He appears to have led, during a long course of years, that most wretched life, the life of an old boy about town. Expensive tastes with little money and licentious appetites with declining vigour, were the just penance for his early irregularities. A severe illness had produced a singular effect on his intellect. His memory played him pranks stranger than almost any that are to be found in the history of that strange faculty. It seemed to be at once preternaturally strong and preternaturally weak. If a book was read to him before he went to bed, he would wake the next morning with his mind full of the thoughts and expressions which he had heard over night; and he would write them down, without in the least suspecting that they were not his own. In his verses the same ideas, and even the same words, came over and over again several times in a short composition. His fine person bore the marks of age, sickness and sorrow; and he mourned for his departed beauty with an effeminate regret. He could not look without a sigh at the portrait which Lely had painted of him when he was only twenty-eight, and often murmured, Quantum mutatus ab illo.

He was still nervously anxious about his literary reputation, and, not content with the fame which he still possessed as a dramatist, was determined to be renowned as a satirist and an amatory poet. In 1704, after twenty-seven years of silence, he again appeared as an author. He put forth a large folio of miscellaneous verses, which, we believe, has never been reprinted. Some of these pieces had probably circulated through the town in manuscript. For, before the volume appeared, the critics at the coffee-houses very confidently predicted that it would be utterly worthless, and were in consequence bitterly reviled by the poet in an ill-written foolish and egotistical preface. The book amply vindicated the most unfavourable prophecies that had been hazarded. The style and versification are beneath criticism; the morals are those of Rochester. For Rochester, indeed, there was some excuse. When his offences against decorum were committed, he was a very young man, misled by a prevailing fashion. Wycherley was sixty-four. He had long outlived the times when libertinism was regarded as essential to the character of a wit and a gentleman. Most of the rising poets, Addison, for example, John Philips and Rowe, were studious of decency. We can hardly conceive anything more miserable than the figure which the ribald old man makes in the midst of so many sober and well-conducted youths.

In the very year in which this bulky volume of obscene doggerel was published, Wycherley formed an acquaintance of a very singular kind. A little, pale, crooked, sickly, bright-eyed urchin, just turned of sixteen, had written some copies of verses in which discerning judges could detect the promise of future eminence. There was, indeed, as yet nothing very striking or original in the conceptions of the young poet. But he was already skilled in the art of metrical composition. His diction and his music were not those of the great old masters; but that which his ablest contemporaries were labouring to do he already did best. His style was not richly poetical; but it was always neat, compact and pointed. His verse wanted variety of pause, of swell and of cadence, but never grated harshly on the ear or disappointed it by a feeble close. The youth was already free of the company of wits, and was greatly elated at being introduced to the author of The Plain Dealer and The Country Wife.

It is curious to trace the history of the intercourse which took place between Wycherley and Pope—between the representative of the age that was going out and the representative of the age that was coming in—between the friend of Rochester and Buckingham and the friend of Lyttleton and Mansfield. At first the boy was enchanted by the kindness and condescension of his new friend, haunted his door and followed him about like a spaniel from coffee-house to coffee-house. Letters full of affection, humility and fulsome flattery were interchanged between the friends. But the first ardour of affection could not last. Pope, though at no time scrupulously delicate in his writings or fastidious as to the morals of his associates, was shocked by the indecency of a rake who, at seventy, was still the representative of the monstrous profligacy of the Restoration. As the youth grew older, as his mind expanded and his fame rose, he appreciated both himself and Wycherley more correctly. He felt a well-founded contempt for the old gentleman's verses, and was at no great pains to conceal his opinion. Wycherley, on the other hand, though blinded by self-love to the imperfections of what he called his poetry, could not but see that there was an immense difference between his young companion's rhymes and his own. He was divided between two feelings. He wished to have the assistance of so skilful a hand to polish his lines; and yet he shrank from the humiliation of being beholden for literary assistance to a lad who might have been his grandson.

Pope was willing to give assistance, but was by no means disposed to give assistance and flattery too. He took the trouble to retouch whole reams of feeble, stumbling verses, and inserted many vigorous lines, which the least skilful reader will distinguish in an instant. But he thought that by these services he acquired a right to express himself in terms which would not, under ordinary circumstances, become one who was addressing a man of four times his age. In one letter, he tells Wycherley that "the worst pieces are such as, to render them very good, would require almost the entire new writing of them." In another, he gives the following account of his corrections: "Though the whole be as short again as at first, there is not one thought omitted but what is a repetition of something in your first volume or in this very paper; and the versification throughout is, I believe, such as nobody can be shocked at. The repeated permission you give me of dealing freely with you, will, I hope, excuse what I have done; for, if I have not spared you when I thought severity would do you a kindness, I have not mangled you when I thought there was no absolute need of amputation."

Wycherley continued to return thanks for all this hacking and hewing, which was, indeed, of inestimable service to his composition. But by degrees his thanks began to sound very like reproaches. In private, he is said to have described Pope as a person who could not cut out a suit, but who had some skill in turning old coats. In his letters to Pope, while he acknowledged that the versification of the poems had been greatly improved, he spoke of the whole art of versification with scorn, and sneered at those who preferred sound to sense. Pope revenged himself for this outbreak of spleen by return of post. He had in his hands a volume of Wycherley's rhymes, and he wrote to say that this volume was so full of faults that he could not correct it without completely defacing the manuscript. "I am," he said, "equally afraid of sparing you and of offending you by too impudent a correction." This was more than flesh and blood could bear. Wycherley reclaimed his papers in a letter in which resentment shows itself plainly through the thin disguise of civility. Pope, glad to be rid of a troublesome and inglorious task, sent back the deposit, and, by way of a parting courtesy, advised the old man to turn his poetry into prose, and assured him that the public would like his thoughts much better without his versification. Thus ended this memorable correspondence.

Wycherley lived some years after the termination of the strange friendship which we have described. The last scene of his life was, perhaps, the most scandalous. Ten days before his death, at seventy-five, he married a young girl, merely in order to injure his nephew, an act which proves that neither years nor adversity, nor what he called his philosophy, nor either of the religions which he had at different times professed, had taught him the rudiments of morality. He died in December, 1715, and lies in the vault under the church of St. Paul in Covent Garden.

His bride soon after married a Captain Shrimpton, who thus became possessed of a large collection of manuscripts. These were sold to a bookseller. They were so full of erasures and interlineations that no printer could decipher them. It was necessary to call in the aid of a professed critic; and Theobald, the editor of Shakespeare and the hero of the first Dunciad, was employed to ascertain the true reading. In this way, a volume of miscellanies in verse and prose was got up for the market. The collection derives all its value from the traces of Pope's hand, which are everywhere discernible.

Of the moral character of Wycherley it can hardly be necessary for us to say more. His fame as a writer rests wholly on his comedies, and chiefly on the last two. Even as a comic writer, he was neither of the best school, nor highest in his school. He was in truth a worst Congreve. His chief merit, like Congreve's, lies in the style of his dialogue. But the wit which lights up The Plain Dealer and The Country Wife is pale and flickering when compared with the gorgeous blaze which dazzles us almost to blindness in Love for Love and The Way of the World. Like Congreve, and, indeed, even more than Congreve, Wycherley is ready to sacrifice dramatic propriety to the liveliness of his dialogue. The poet speaks out of the mouths of all his dunces and coxcombs, and makes them describe themselves with a good sense and acuteness which puts them on a level with the wits and heroes. We will give two instances, the first which occur to us, from The Country Wife. There are in the world fools who find the society of old friends insipid and who are always running after new companions. Such a character is a fair subject for comedy. But nothing can be more absurd than to introduce a man of this sort saying to his comrade, "I can deny you nothing: for though I have known thee a great while, never go if I do not love thee as well as a new acquaintance." That town-wits again, have always been rather a heartless class, is true. But none of them, we will answer for it, ever said to a young lady to whom he was making love, "We wits rail and make love often but to show our parts: as we have no affections, so we have no malice."

Wycherley's plays are said to have been the produce of long and patient labour. The epithet of "slow" was early given to him by Rochester, and was frequently repeated. In truth, his mind, unless we are greatly mistaken, was naturally a very meagre soil, and was forced only by great labour and outlay to bear fruit which, after all, was not of the highest flavour. He has scarcely more claim to originality than Terence. It is not too much to say that there is hardly anything of the least value in his plays of which the hint is not to be found elsewhere. The best scenes in The Gentleman Dancing-Master were suggested by Calderon's Maestro de Danzar, not by any means one of the happiest comedies of the great Castilian poet. The Country Wife is borrowed from the Ecole des Maris and the Ecole des Femmes. The groundwork of The Plain Dealer is taken from the Misanthrope of Molière. One whole scene is almost translated from the Critique de l'Ecole des Femmes. Fidelia is Shakespeare's Viola stolen, and marred in the stealing: and the widow Blackacre, beyond comparison Wycherley's best comic character, is the Countess in Racine's Plaideurs, talking the jargon of English instead of that of French chicane.

The only thing original about Wycherley, the only thing which he could furnish from his own mind in inexhaustible abundance, was profligacy. It is curious to observe how everything that he touched, however pure and noble, took in an instant the colour of his own mind. Compare the Ecole des Femmes with The Country Wife. Agnes is a simple and amiable girl, whose heart is indeed full of love, but of love sanctioned by honour, morality and religion. Her natural talents are great. They have been hidden and, as it might appear, destroyed by an education elaborately bad. But they are called forth into full energy by a virtuous passion. Her lover, while he adores her beauty, is too honest a man to abuse the confiding tenderness of a creature so charming and inexperienced. Wycherley takes this plot into his hands; and forthwith this sweet and graceful courtship becomes a licentious intrigue of the lowest and least sentimental kind, between an impudent London rake and the idiot wife of a country squire. We will not go into details. In truth, Wycherley's indecency is protected against the critics as a skunk is protected against the hunters. It is safe, because it is too filthy to handle and too noisome even to approach.

It is the same with The Plain Dealer. How careful has Shakespeare been in Twelfth Night to preserve the dignity and delicacy of Viola under her disguise! Even when wearing a page's doublet and hose, she is never mixed up with any transaction which the most fastidious mind could regard as leaving a stain on her. She is employed by the Duke on an embassy of love to Olivia, but on an embassy of the most honourable kind. Wycherley borrows Viola—and Viola forthwith becomes a pander of the basest sort. But the character of Manly is the best illustration of our meaning. Molière exhibited in his misanthrope a pure and noble mind which had been sorely vexed by the sight of perfidy and malevolence disguised under the forms of politeness. As every extreme naturally generates its contrary, Alceste adopts a standard of good and evil directly opposed to that of the society which surrounds him. Courtesy seems to him a vice; and those stern virtues which are neglected by the fops and coquettes of Paris become too exclusively the objects of his veneration. He is often to blame; he is often ridiculous: but he is always a good man; and the feeling which he inspires is regret that a person so estimable should be so unamiable. Wycherley borrowed Alceste, and turned him—we quote the words of so lenient a critic as Mr. Leigh Hunt—into "a ferocious sensualist, who believed himself as great a rascal as he thought everybody else." The surliness of Molière's hero is copied and caricatured. But the most nauseous libertinism and the most dastardly fraud are substituted for the purity and integrity of the original. And, to make the whole complete, Wycherley does not seem to have been aware that he was not drawing the portrait of an eminently honest man. So depraved was his moral taste, that, while he firmly believed that he was producing a picture of virtue too exalted for the commerce of this world, he was really delineating the greatest rascal that is to be found even in his own writings.

LOVE IN A WOOD; or ST. JAMES'S PARK

—*Excludit sanos Helicone poetas*
Democritus.—HORAT.

Wycherley informed Pope that he wrote his first comedy. Love in a Wood, at the age of nineteen—i.e. in the year 1659-60. If this statement be accurate, the play must have undergone very considerable alterations previous to its production on the stage; for not only do we discover in it occasional allusions to events of later years, but the whole piece displays an intimate acquaintance with life in the metropolis scarcely commensurate with the opportunities of a youth who, from the age of fifteen, when he was sent into France, to that of twenty, when he became a student at Oxford, can have passed but a few weeks, at the most, in London. From the Biographia Britannica we learn that Wycherley returned from France shortly before the Restoration; from Wood's Athenæ Oxonienses that he became a fellow commoner of Queen's College, Oxford, also "a little before the Restoration of Charles II., but wore not a gown, only lived in the provost's lodgings," and "was entered in the public library (the Bodleian) under the title of philosophiæ studiosus in July, 1660." In the Fasti Oxonienses, however, the following entry occurs under the year 1660: "In the month of July this year Will. Wicherley became sojourner in Oxon for the sake of the public library." We are at liberty, therefore, to conclude that between the date of his return to England and the following July, part, at least, of our author's time may have been spent in London, where he may possibly have composed the first draught of his comedy, and where, at all events, his quick observation would furnish him with material sufficient for a first draught.

The year 1672 has been universally determined as that of the first performance of Love in a Wood; I believe, nevertheless, incorrectly. We are as certain as we can be, in the absence of direct evidence, that Wycherley's second play, The Gentleman Dancing-Master, was first brought upon the stage in 1671. Now there is little doubt that The Gentleman Dancing-Master had been preceded by Love in a Wood, for not only do the authorities generally concur in assigning an earlier date to the production of the latter play, but Wycherley, in dedicating it to the Duchess of Cleveland, refers pointedly to himself as a "new author." Further in the dedication we find that her Grace had honoured the poet by going to see his comedy twice together, during Lent, and had been pleased, thereupon, to command from him a copy of the play, with which he takes occasion to offer the dedicatory epistle. These were not the days of long runs, even for the most successful dramas, nor are we likely to err in assuming that the Duchess was present at an early performance of the piece which she distinguished with her favour; or that Wycherley prefixed her title to a comedy newly brought upon the stage, rather than to one which had already been for some time the property of the public, and which had been revived, as must then have been the case, before the Duchess had seen it. Note, also, that the dedication is addressed to the Duchess of Cleveland by that title. In Lent, 1670, Barbara Palmer was Countess of Castlemaine: she was created Duchess of Cleveland on the 3rd of August in the same year. Considering then that the piece was certainly performed during Lent, that it cannot have been produced later than 1671, and that the Duchess to whom it was inscribed enjoyed not that title until the autumn of 1670, we may conclude, with tolerable security, that the first performance of Love in a Wood took place some time during the spring of 1671.

Genest indeed, supposes it to have been brought out by the King's Company after their removal to the theatre in Lincoln's Inn Fields. Their own house in Drury Lane having been destroyed by fire in January, 1672, they opened, on the 26th of February following, the Lincoln's Inn Fields Theatre, which had been untenanted since the migration of the Duke's Company to Dorset Gardens in the preceding November, with a representation of Beaumont and Fletcher's Wit without Money. This was succeeded, in order, by Arviragus and Philicia and Dryden's Marriage à la Mode, after which, Genest thinks, Love in a Wood was produced. But, on this supposition, the first performance of Love in a Wood must have taken place later than that of The Gentleman Dancing-Master, and in that case it seems hardly probable that Wycherley should describe himself as a new author in the dedication to the former play. Moreover, the prologue to Wycherley's third comedy, The Country Wife, contains a distinct allusion to the recent ill-fortune of The Gentleman Dancing-Master, which we can scarcely suppose the author would have thus referred to, had a successful play of his been produced in the interval, and that by the same company which brought forward The Country Wife. In fact, the only argument which I can conceive it possible to adduce in support of Genest must be based upon a conjecture that not only The Gentleman Dancing-Master, but Love in a Wood also, had failed to win the favour of the public, and that it is the latter play to which allusion is intended in the prologue to The Country Wife. That The Gentleman Dancing-Master proved a failure is certain; that Love in a Wood succeeded, we have no direct evidence, but of circumstantial sufficient, I think, to prove the point. The general assumption in its favour we may pass; but the whole tone of the dedication, though it afford us no information, in so many words, as to the fate of the piece, forbids us to believe that it can have been indited by the "baffled scribbler" of a condemned comedy. Indeed, had the piece thus failed, it is quite inconceivable that Wycherley would have had the temerity to offer it to the Duchess; he would rather have sent it into the world silently, and without the flourish of a dedication, as was actually the case with The Gentleman Dancing-Master. Dennis, moreover, declares expressly that Love in a Wood brought its author acquainted with the wits of the Court, and we may question whether the reputation of an unprosperous playwright would have proved the surest passport to their intimacy.

The reasons for rejecting the date of 1672 thus recounted, there remains but to notice one inconsiderable particular, which, could we allow it consequence, would tend to determine the production of Love in a Wood at a yet earlier date than that to which I have assigned it. In a conversation with the Duchess, immediately after her visit to his play, Wycherley, as reported by Dennis, continually addresses her Grace by the title of "your Ladyship." I doubt not, however, that this is a mere slip on the part of Dennis, nor can we easily imagine that Wycherley deferred, until the autumn, the presentation of his play to a lady who had "commanded" it of him, with such distinguishing marks of favour, in the preceding spring.

Love in a Wood, then, was produced by the King's company, during the spring of 1671, at the Theatre Royal, in Drury Lane. Some of the first actors of the day took part in the performances. Hart, who in tragedy yielded the palm to Betterton alone, appeared as Ranger, Mohun as Dapperwit; Lacy the comedian, soon afterwards "creator" of Bayes, as Alderman Gripe; and Kinaston, who in his youth, before women trod the boards, had been famous in female parts, now, changing sides, enacted the jealous lover, Valentine. The rôle of Lady Flippant was taken by an actress well known to us from the pages of Pepys—his favourite Mrs. Knipp, "a merry jade!"

Upon the whole this play must be owned inferior to Wycherley's other dramas. It is excelled in unity of action by The Gentleman Dancing-Master, in richness of humour by The Country Wife, in strength of satire by The Plain Dealer. Nevertheless, it is a highly diverting, witty comedy, and strikingly superior to most of the new plays which, since the Restoration, had preceded it upon the stage. Some critics would have us believe that Wycherley derived the suggestion of this play from Sir Charles Sedley's comedy of The Mulberry Garden. It is difficult to understand upon what grounds this assertion is based. In the first place, although The Mulberry Garden was produced on the stage in 1668, nearly three years earlier than Love in a Wood, it is exceedingly doubtful if it were earlier written. Indeed, if Wycherley may be credited as to the year in which his own play was composed, the question of priority is easily settled, for The Mulberry Garden cannot have been written until after the Restoration, as its dénouement turns upon the proclamation of the King by General Monk. Moreover, it is hardly possible that Wycherley should have known anything of Sedley's play before its public representation, as he seems not to have been acquainted with Sedley himself until after the production of his own drama, so that our acceptance of the theory that he borrowed from Sedley the hint of Love in a Wood would involve the unwarrantable conclusion that he also, in conversation with Pope, antedated its composition by at least eight years. But further, the only considerable point of resemblance between the two plays appears to be that while in Wycherley's part of the action takes place in St. James's Park, in Sedley's one of the scenes is laid in the Mulberry Garden, which was certainly very near to St. James's Park, being, in fact, situated at its western extremity. If the reader choose to consider this remarkable coincidence sufficient to justify a charge of plagiarism against Wycherley, I have nothing more to urge in his defence.

Love in a Wood was registered at Stationers' Hall on the 6th of October, 1671, and was published in the following year.

TO HER GRACE THE DUCHESS OF CLEVELAND

Madam,

All authors whatever in their dedication are poets; but I am now to write to a lady who stands as little in need of flattery, as her beauty of art; otherwise I should prove as ill a poet to her in my dedication, as to my reader in my play. I can do your Grace no honour, nor make you more admirers than you have already; yet I can do myself the honour to let the world know I am the greatest you have. You will pardon me, Madam, for you know it is very hard for a new author, and poet too, to govern his ambition: for poets, let them pass in the world ever so much for modest, honest men, but begin praise to others which concludes in themselves; and are like rooks, who lend people money but to win it back again, and so leave them in debt to 'em for nothing; they offer laurel and incense to their heroes, but wear it themselves, and perfume themselves. This is true, Madam, upon the honest word of an author who never yet writ dedication. Yet though I cannot lie like them, I am as vain as they; and cannot but publicly give your Grace my humble acknowledgments for the favours I have received from you:—this, I say, is the poet's gratitude, which, in plain English, is only pride and ambition; and that the world might know your Grace did me the honour to see my play twice together. Yet, perhaps, my enviers of your favour will suggest 'twas in Lent, and therefore for your mortification. Then, as a jealous author, I am concerned not to have your Grace's favours lessened, or rather my reputation; and to let them know, you were pleased, after that, to command a copy from me of this play;—the only way, without beauty and wit, to win a poor poet's heart.

'Tis a sign your Grace understands nothing better than obliging all the world after the best and most proper manner. But, Madam, to be obliging to that excess as you are (pardon me, if I tell you, out of my extreme concern and service for your Grace) is a dangerous quality, and may be very incommode to you; for civility makes poets as troublesome, as charity makes beggars; and your Grace will be hereafter as much pestered with such scurvy offerings as this, poems, panegyrics, and the like, as you are now with petitions: and, Madam, take it from me, no man with papers in 's hand is more dreadful than a poet; no, not a lawyer with his declarations. Your Grace sure did not well consider what ye did, in sending for my play: you little thought I would have had the confidence to send you a dedication too. But, Madam, you find I am as unreasonable, and have as little conscience, as if I had driven the poetic trade longer than I have, and ne'er consider you had enough of the play. But (having suffered now so severely) I beseech your Grace, have a care for the future; take my counsel, and be (if you can possible) as proud and ill-natured as other people of quality, since your quiet is so much concerned, and since you have more reason than any to value yourself:—for you have that perfection of beauty (without thinking it so) which others of your sex but think they have; that generosity in your actions which others of your quality have only in their promises; that spirit, wit and judgment, and all other qualifications which fit heroes to command, and would make any but your Grace proud. I begin now, elevated by my subject, to write with the emotion and fury of a poet, yet the integrity of an historian; and I could never be weary—nay, sure this were my only way to make my readers never weary too, though they were a more impatient generation of people than they are. In fine, speaking thus of your Grace, I should please all the world but you; therefore I must once observe and obey you against my will, and say no more, than that I am,

Madam,
Your Grace's most obliged, and most humble servant,
WILLIAM WYCHERLEY.

DRAMATIS PERSONÆ

MR RANGER, **MR VINCENT**, **MR VALENTINE**, Young Gentlemen of the town.
Alderman **GRIPE**, seemingly precise, but a covetous, lecherous, old Usurer of the city.
SIR SIMON ADDLEPLOT, a Coxcomb, always in pursuit of women of great fortunes.
MR DAPPERWIT, a brisk, conceited, half-witted fellow of the town.
Mrs. Crossbite's **LANDLORD**, and his **PRENTICES**, **SERVANTS**, **WAITERS**, and other **ATTENDANTS**.
CHRISTINA, Valentine's Mistress.
LYDIA, Ranger's Mistress.
LADY FLIPPANT, Gripe's sister, an affected Widow in distress for a husband, though still declaiming against marriage.
MRS MARTHA, Gripe's Daughter.
MRS JOYNER, a Match-maker, or precise city bawd.
MRS CROSSBITE, an old cheating jill, and bawd to her Daughter.
MISS LUCY, Mrs. Crossbite's Daughter.
ISABEL, Christina's Woman.
LEONORE, Servant to Lydia.

SCENE:—**LONDON**

PROLOGUE

Custom, which bids the thief from cart harangue
All those that come to make and see him hang,
Wills the damned poet (though he knows he's gone)
To greet you ere his execution.
Not having fear of critic 'fore his eyes,
But still rejecting wholesome, good advice,
He e'en is come to suffer here to-day
For counterfeiting (as you judge) a play,
Which is against dread Phœbus highest treason;
Damn, damning judges, therefore, you have reason:—
You he does mean who, for the selfsame fault,
That damning privilege of yours have bought.
So the huge bankers, when they needs must fail,
Send the small brothers of their trade to jail;
Whilst they, by breaking, gentlemen are made,
Then, more than any, scorn poor men o' the trade.

You hardened renegado poets, who
Treat rhyming poets worse than Turk would do,
But vent your heathenish rage, hang, draw, and quarter;
His Muse will die to-day a fleering martyr;
Since for bald jest, dull libel, or lampoon,
There are who suffer persecution
With the undaunted briskness of buffoon,
And strict professors live of raillery,
Defying porter's-lodge, or pillory.
For those who yet write on our poet's fate,
Should as co-sufferers commiserate:
But he in vain their pity now would crave,
Who for themselves, alas! no pity have,
And their own gasping credit will not save;

And those, much less, our criminal would spare,
Who ne'er in rhyme transgress;—if such there are.
Well then, who nothing hopes, need nothing fear:
And he, before your cruel votes shall do it,
By his despair declares himself no poet.

LOVE IN A WOOD; or, ST. JAMES'S PARK

ACT THE FIRST

SCENE I.—Gripe's House, in the evening

Enter **LADY FLIPPANT** and **MRS JOYNER**.

LADY FLIPPANT
Not a husband to be had for money!—Come, come, I might have been a better housewife for myself, as the world goes now, if I had dealt for an heir with his guardian, uncle, or mother-in-law; and you are no better than a chouse, a cheat.

MRS JOYNER
I a cheat, madam!

LADY FLIPPANT
I am out of my money, and patience too.

MRS JOYNER
Do not run out of your patience, whatever you do:—'tis a necessary virtue for a widow without a jointure, in truly.

LADY FLIPPANT

Vile woman! though my fortune be something wasted, my person's in good repair. If I had not depended on you, I had had a husband before this time. When I gave you the last five pounds, did you not promise I should be married by Christmas?

MRS JOYNER
And I had kept my promise if you had co-operated.

LADY FLIPPANT
Co-operated! what should I have done? 'Tis well known no woman breathing could use more industry to get her a husband than I have. Has not my husband's 'scutcheon walked as much ground as the citizens' signs since the Fire?—that no quarter of the town might be ignorant of the widow Flippant.

MRS JOYNER
'Tis well known, madam, indeed.

LADY FLIPPANT
Have I not owned myself (against my stomach) the relict of a citizen, to credit my fortune?

MRS JOYNER
'Tis confessed, madam.

LADY FLIPPANT
Have I not constantly kept Covent-Garden church, St. Martin's, the playhouses, Hyde Park, Mulberry garden, and all the other public marts where widows and maids are exposed?

MRS JOYNER
Far be it from me to think you have an aversion to a husband. But why, madam, have you refused so many good offers?

LADY FLIPPANT
Good offers, Mrs. Joyner! I'll be sworn I never had an offer since my late husband's.—If I had an offer, Mrs. Joyner!—there's the thing, Mrs. Joyner.

MRS JOYNER
Then your frequent and public detestation of marriage is thought real; and if you have had no offer, there's the thing, madam.

LADY FLIPPANT
I cannot deny but I always rail against marriage;—which is the widow's way to it certainly.

MRS JOYNER
'Tis the desperate way of the desperate widows, in truly.

LADY FLIPPANT
Would you have us as tractable as the wenches that eat oatmeal, and fooled like them too?

MRS JOYNER

If nobody were wiser than I, I should think, since the widow wants the natural allurement which the virgin has, you ought to give men all other encouragements, in truly.

LADY FLIPPANT
Therefore, on the contrary, because the widow's fortune (whether supposed or real) is her chiefest bait, the more chary she seems of it, and the more she withdraws it, the more eagerly the busy gaping fry will bite. With us widows, husbands are got like bishoprics, by saying "No:" and I tell you, a young heir is as shy of a widow as of a rook, to my knowledge.

MRS JOYNER
I can allege nothing against your practice—but your ill success; and indeed you must use another method with Sir Simon Addleplot.

LADY FLIPPANT
Will he be at your house at the hour?

MRS JOYNER
He'll be there by ten:—'tis now nine. I'll warrant you he will not fail.

LADY FLIPPANT
I'll warrant you then I will not fail:—for 'tis more than time I were sped.

MRS JOYNER
Mr. Dapperwit has not been too busy with you, I hope?—Your experience has taught you to prevent a mischance.

LADY FLIPPANT
No, no, my mischance (as you call it) is greater than that. I have but three months to reckon, ere I lie down with my port and equipage, and must be delivered of a woman, a footman, and a coachman:—for my coach must down, unless I can get Sir Simon to draw with me.

MRS JOYNER [Aside]
He will pair with you exactly if you knew all.

LADY FLIPPANT
Ah, Mrs. Joyner, nothing grieves me like the putting down my coach! For the fine clothes, the fine lodgings,—let 'em go; for a lodging is as unnecessary a thing to a widow that has a coach, as a hat to a man that has a good peruke. For, as you see about town, she is most properly at home in her coach:—she eats, and drinks, and sleeps in her coach; and for her visits, she receives them in the playhouse.

MRS JOYNER
Ay, ay, let the men keep lodgings, as you say, madam, if they will.

[Enter behind, at one door, **GRIPE** and **SIR SIMON ADDLEPLOT**, the latter in the dress of a Clerk; at the other, **MRS MARTHA**.

LADY FLIPPANT

Do you think if things had been with me as they have been, I would ever have housed with this counter-fashion brother of mine, (who hates a vest as much as a surplice,) to have my patches assaulted every day at dinner, my freedom censured, and my visitants shut out of doors?—Poor Mr. Dapperwit cannot be admitted.

MRS JOYNER
He knows him too well to keep his acquaintance.

LADY FLIPPANT
He is a censorious rigid fop, and knows nothing.

GRIPE [Behind]
So, so!

MRS JOYNER [Aside]
Is he here?—
[To **LADY FLIPPANT**]
Nay, with your pardon, madam, I must contradict you there. He is a prying commonwealth's-man, an implacable magistrate, a sturdy pillar of his cause, and—
[To **GRIPE**]
But, oh me, is your worship so near then? if I had thought you heard me—

GRIPE
Why, why, Mrs. Joyner, I have said as much of myself ere now; and without vanity, I profess.

MRS JOYNER
I know your virtue is proof against vainglory; but the truth to your face looks like flattery in your worship's servant.

GRIPE
No, no; say what you will of me in that kind, far be it from me to suspect you of flattery.

MRS JOYNER
In truly, your worship knows yourself, and knows me, for I am none of those—

LADY FLIPPANT [Aside]
Now they are in—Mrs. Joyner, I'll go before to your house, you'll be sure to come after me.

MRS JOYNER
Immediately.—

[Exit **LADY FLIPPANT**.

But as I was saying, I am none of those—

GRIPE
No, Mrs. Joyner, you cannot sew pillows under folks' elbows; you cannot hold a candle to the devil; you cannot tickle a trout to take him; you—

MRS JOYNER
Lord, how well you do know me indeed!—and you shall see I know your worship as well. You cannot backslide from your principles; you cannot be terrified by the laws; nor bribed to allegiance by office or preferment; you—

GRIPE
Hold, hold, my praise must not interrupt yours.

MRS JOYNER
With your worship's pardon, in truly, I must on.

GRIPE
I am full of your praise, and it will run over.

MRS JOYNER
Nay, sweet sir, you are—

GRIPE
Nay, sweet Mrs. Joyner, you are—

MRS JOYNER
Nay, good your worship, you are—

[Stops her mouth with his handkerchief.

GRIPE
I say you are—

MRS JOYNER
I must not be rude with your worship.

GRIPE
You are a nursing mother to the saints; through you they gather together; through you they fructify and increase; and through you the child cries from out of the hand-basket.

MRS JOYNER
Through you virgins are married, or provided for as well; through you the reprobate's wife is made a saint; and through you the widow is not disconsolate, nor misses her husband.

GRIPE
Through you—

MRS JOYNER
Indeed you will put me to the blush.

GRIPE

Blushes are badges of imperfection:—saints have no shame. You are—are the flower of matrons, Mrs. Joyner.

MRS JOYNER
You are the pink of courteous aldermen.

GRIPE
You are the muffler of secrecy.

MRS JOYNER
You are the head-band of justice.

GRIPE
Thank you, sweet Mrs. Joyner: do you think so indeed? You are—you are the bonfire of devotion.

MRS JOYNER
You are the bellows of zeal.

GRIPE
You are the cupboard of charity.

MRS JOYNER
You are the fob of liberality.

GRIPE
You are the rivet of sanctified love or wedlock.

MRS JOYNER
You are the picklock and dark-lantern of policy; and, in a word, a conventicle of virtues.

GRIPE
Your servant, your servant, sweet Mrs. Joyner! you have stopped my mouth.

MRS JOYNER
Your servant, your servant, sweet alderman! I have nothing to say.

SIR SIMON ADDLEPLOT
The half pullet will be cold, sir.

GRIPE
Mrs. Joyner, you shall sup with me.

MRS JOYNER
Indeed I am engaged to supper with some of your man's friends; and I came on purpose to get leave for him too.

GRIPE

I cannot deny you anything. But I have forgot to tell you what a kind of fellow my sister's Dapperwit is: before a full table of the coffee-house sages, he had the impudence to hold an argument against me in the defence of vests and protections; and therefore I forbid him my house; besides, when he came I was forced to lock up my daughter for fear of him, nay, I think the poor child herself was afraid of him.—Come hither, child, were you not afraid of Dapperwit?

MRS MARTHA [Aside]
Yes indeed, sir, he is a terrible man.—Yet I durst meet with him in a piazza at midnight.

GRIPE
He shall never come into my doors again.

MRS MARTHA
Shall Mr. Dapperwit never come hither again then?

GRIPE
No, child.

MRS MARTHA
I am afraid he will.

GRIPE
I warrant thee.

MRS MARTHA [Aside]
I warrant you then I'll go to him.—I am glad of that, for I hate him as much as a bishop.

GRIPE
Thou art no child of mine, if thou dost not hate bishops and wits.—Well, Mrs. Joyner, I'll keep you no longer.
[To **SIR SIMON ADDLEPLOT**]
Jonas, wait on Mrs. Joyner.

MRS JOYNER
Good night to your worship.

GRIPE
But stay, stay, Mrs. Joyner: have you spoken with the widow Crossbite about her little daughter, as I desired?

MRS JOYNER
I will to-morrow early; it shall be the first thing I'll do after my prayers.

GRIPE
If Dapperwit should contaminate her!—I cannot rest till I have redeemed her from the jaws of that lion.—Good night.

MRS JOYNER

Good gentleman.

Exeunt **GRIPE** *and* **MRS MARTHA**.

SIR SIMON ADDLEPLOT
Ha! ha! ha! Mrs. Joyner.

MRS JOYNER
What's the matter, Sir Simon?

SIR SIMON ADDLEPLOT
Ha! ha! ha!—let us make haste to your house, or I shall burst, faith and troth, to see what fools you and I make of these people.

MRS JOYNER
I will not rob you of any of the credit; I am but a feeble instrument, you are an engineer.

SIR SIMON ADDLEPLOT
Remember what you say now when things succeed, and do not tell me then,—I must thank your wit for all.

MRS JOYNER
No, in truly, Sir Simon.

SIR SIMON ADDLEPLOT
Nay, I am sure Dapperwit and I have been partners in many an intrigue, and he uses to serve me so.

MRS JOYNER
He is an ill man to intrigue with, as you call it.

SIR SIMON ADDLEPLOT
Ay, so are all your wits; a pox! if a man's understanding be not so public as theirs, he cannot do a wise action but they go away with the honour of it, if he be of their acquaintance.

MRS JOYNER
Why do you keep such acquaintance then?

SIR SIMON ADDLEPLOT
There is a proverb, Mrs. Joyner, "You may know him by his company."

MRS JOYNER
No, no, to be thought a man of parts, you must always keep company with a man of less wit than yourself.

SIR SIMON ADDLEPLOT
That's the hardest thing in the world for me to do, faith and troth.

MRS JOYNER

What, to find a man of less wit than yourself? Pardon my raillery, Sir Simon.

SIR SIMON ADDLEPLOT
No, no, I cannot keep company with a fool:—I wonder how men of parts can do't, there's something in't.

MRS JOYNER
If you could, all your wise actions would be your own, and your money would be your own too.

SIR SIMON ADDLEPLOT
Nay, faith and troth, that's true; for your wits are plaguily given to borrow. They'll borrow of their wench, coachman, or linkboy, their hire, Mrs. Joyner; Dapperwit has that trick with a vengeance.

MRS JOYNER
Why will you keep company with him then, I say? for, to be plain with you, you have followed him so long, that you are thought but his cully; for every wit has his cully, as every squire his led captain.

SIR SIMON ADDLEPLOT
I his cully, I his cully, Mrs. Joyner! Lord, that I should be thought a cully to any wit breathing!

MRS JOYNER
Nay, do not take it so to heart, for the best wits of the town are but cullies themselves.

SIR SIMON ADDLEPLOT
To whom, to whom, to whom, Mrs. Joyner?

MRS JOYNER
To sempstresses and bawds.

SIR SIMON ADDLEPLOT
To your knowledge, Mrs. Joyner.—
[Aside]
There I was with her.

MRS JOYNER
To tailors and vintners, but especially to the French houses.

SIR SIMON ADDLEPLOT
But Dapperwit is a cully to none of them; for he ticks.

MRS JOYNER
I care not, but I wish you were a cully to none but me; that's all the hurt I wish you.

SIR SIMON ADDLEPLOT
Thank you, Mrs. Joyner. Well, I will throw off Dapperwit's acquaintance when I am married, and will only be a cully to my wife; and that's no more than the wisest husband of 'em all is.

MRS JOYNER
Then you think you shall carry Mrs. Martha?

SIR SIMON ADDLEPLOT
Your hundred guineas are as good as in your lap.

MRS JOYNER
But I am afraid this double plot of yours should fail: you would sooner succeed if you only designed upon Mrs. Martha, or only upon my Lady Flippant.

SIR SIMON ADDLEPLOT
Nay, then, you are no woman of intrigue, faith and troth: 'tis good to have two strings to one's bow. If Mrs. Martha be coy, I tell the widow I put on my disguise for her; but if Mrs. Martha be kind to Jonas, Sir Simon Addleplot will be false to the widow: which is no more than widows are used to; for a promise to a widow is as seldom kept as a vow made at sea, as Dapperwit says.

MRS JOYNER
I am afraid they should discover you.

SIR SIMON ADDLEPLOT
You have nothing to fear; you have your twenty guineas in your pocket for helping me into my service, and if I get into Mrs. Martha's quarters, you have a hundred more; if into the widow's, fifty:—happy go lucky! Will her ladyship be at your house at the hour?

MRS JOYNER
Yes.

SIR SIMON ADDLEPLOT
Then you shall see when I am Sir Simon Addleplot and myself I'll look like myself; now I am Jonas, I look like an ass. You never thought Sir Simon Addleplot could have looked so like an ass by his ingenuity.

MRS JOYNER
Pardon me, Sir Simon.

SIR SIMON ADDLEPLOT
Nay, do not flatter, faith and troth.

MRS JOYNER
Come let us go, 'tis time.

SIR SIMON ADDLEPLOT
I will carry the widow to the French house.

MRS JOYNER
If she will go.

SIR SIMON ADDLEPLOT
If she will go! why, did you ever know a widow refuse a treat? no more than a lawyer a fee, faith and troth: yet I know too—

No treat, sweet words, good mien, but sly intrigue   That must at length the jilting widow fegue.

[Exeunt.

SCENE II.—The French House

A table, wine and candles.

Enter **VINCENT**, **RANGER**, and **DAPPERWIT**.

DAPPERWIT
Pray, Mr. Ranger, let's have no drinking to-night.

VINCENT
Pray, Mr. Ranger, let's have no Dapperwit to-night.

RANGER
Nay, nay, Vincent.

VINCENT
A pox! I hate his impertinent chat more than he does the honest Burgundy.

DAPPERWIT
But why should you force wine upon us? we are not all of your gusto.

VINCENT
But why should you force your chawed jests, your damned ends of your mouldy lampoons, and last year's sonnets, upon us? we are not all of your gusto.

DAPPERWIT
The wine makes me sick, let me perish!

VINCENT
Thy rhymes make me spew.

RANGER
At repartee already! Come, Vincent. I know you would rather have him pledge you: here, Dapperwit—

[Gives him the glass.

—But why are you so eager to have him drink always?

VINCENT
Because he is so eager to talk always, and there is no other way to silence him.

[Enter **WAITER**.

WAITER
Here is a gentleman desires to speak with Mr. Vincent.

VINCENT
I come.

[Exit VINCENT with WAITER.

DAPPERWIT
He may drink, because he is obliged to the bottle for all the wit and courage he has; 'tis not free and natural like yours.

RANGER
He has more courage than wit, but wants neither.

DAPPERWIT
As a pump gone dry, if you pour no water down you will get none out, so—

RANGER
Nay, I bar similes too, to-night.

DAPPERWIT
Why, is not the thought new? don't you apprehend it?

RANGER
Yes, yes, but—

DAPPERWIT
Well, well, will you comply with his sottishness too, and hate brisk things in complaisance to the ignorant dull age? I believe shortly 'twill be as hard to find a patient friend to communicate one's wit to, as a faithful friend to communicate one's secret to. Wit has as few true judges as painting, I see.

RANGER
All people pretend to be judges of both.

DAPPERWIT
Ay, they pretend; but set you aside, and one or two more—

RANGER
But why, has Vincent neither courage nor wit?

DAPPERWIT
He has no courage, because he beat his wench for giving me les doux yeux once; and no wit, because he does not comprehend my thoughts; and he is a son of a whore for his ignorance. I take ignorance worse from any man than the lie, because 'tis as much as to say I am no wit.

[Re-enter VINCENT.

You need not take any notice, though, to him what I say.

VINCENT
Ranger, there is a woman below in a coach would speak with you.

RANGER
With me?

[Exit **RANGER**.

DAPPERWIT
This Ranger, Mr. Vincent, is as false to his friend as his wench.

VINCENT
You have no reason to say so, but because he is absent.

DAPPERWIT
'Tis disobliging to tell a man of his faults to his face. If he had but your grave parts and manly wit, I should adore him; but, a pox! he is a mere buffoon, a jack-pudding, let me perish!

VINCENT
You are an ungrateful fellow. I have heard him maintain you had wit, which was more than e'er you could do for yourself.—I thought you had owned him your Mæcenas.

DAPPERWIT
A pox! he cannot but esteem me, 'tis for his honour; but I cannot but be just for all that—without favour or affection. Yet I confess I love him so well, that I wish he had but the hundredth part of your courage.

VINCENT
He has had courage to save you from many a beating, to my knowledge.

DAPPERWIT
Come, come, I wish the man well, and, next to you, better than any man! and, I am sorry to say it, he has not courage to snuff a candle with his fingers. When he is drunk, indeed, he dares get a clap, or so—and swear at a constable.

VINCENT
Detracting fop! when did you see him desert his friend?

DAPPERWIT
You have a rough kind of a raillery, Mr. Vincent; but since you will have it, (though I love the man heartily, I say,) he deserted me once in breaking of windows, for fear of the constables—

[Re-enter **RANGER**.

But you need not take notice to him of what I tell you; I hate to put a man to the blush.

RANGER
I have had just now a visit from my mistress, who is as jealous of me as a wife of her husband when she lies in:—my cousin Lydia,—you have heard me speak of her.

VINCENT
But she is more troublesome than a wife that lies in, because she follows you to your haunts. Why do you allow her that privilege before her time?

RANGER
Faith, I may allow her any privilege, and be too hard for her yet. How do you think I have cheated her to-night?—Women are poor credulous creatures, easily deceived.

VINCENT
We are poor credulous creatures, when we think 'em so.

RANGER
Intending a ramble to St. James's Park to-night, upon some probable hopes of some fresh game I have in chase, I appointed her to stay at home; with a promise to come to her within this hour, that she might not spoil the scent and prevent my sport.

VINCENT
She'll be even with you when you are married, I warrant you. In the meantime here's her health, Dapperwit.

RANGER
Now had he rather be at the window, writing her anagram in the glass with his diamond, or biting his nails in the corner for a fine thought to come and divert us with at the table.

DAPPERWIT
No, a pox! I have no wit to-night. I am as barren and hide-bound as one of your damned scribbling poets, who are sots in company for all their wit; as a miser is poor for all his money. How do you like the thought?

VINCENT
Drink, drink!

DAPPERWIT
Well, I can drink this, because I shall be reprieved presently.

VINCENT
Who will be so civil to us?

DAPPERWIT
Sir Simon Addleplot:—I have bespoke him a supper here, for he treats to-night a new rich mistress.

RANGER
That spark, who has his fruitless designs upon the bed-ridden rich widow, down to the suckling heiress in her pissing-clout. He was once the sport, but now the public grievance, of all the fortunes in town; for

he watches them like a younger brother that is afraid to be mumped of his snip, and they cannot steal a marriage, nor stay their stomachs, but he must know it.

DAPPERWIT
He has now pitched his nets for Gripe's daughter, the rich scrivener, and serves him as a clerk to get admission to her; which the watchful fop her father denies to all others.

RANGER
I thought you had been nibbling at her once, under pretence of love to her aunt.

DAPPERWIT
I confess I have the same design yet, and Addleplot is but my agent, whilst he thinks me his. He brings me letters constantly from her, and carries mine back.

VINCENT
Still betraying your best friends!

DAPPERWIT
I cannot in honour but betray him. Let me perish! the poor young wench is taken with my person, and would scratch through four walls to come to me.

VINCENT
'Tis a sign she is kept up close indeed.

DAPPERWIT
Betray him! I'll not be traitor to love for any man.

[Enter **SIR SIMON ADDLEPLOT** with the **WAITER**.

SIR SIMON ADDLEPLOT
Know 'em! you are a saucy Jack-straw to question me, faith and troth; I know everybody, and everybody knows me.

ALL
Sir Simon! Sir Simon! Sir Simon!

RANGER
And you are a welcome man to everybody.

SIR SIMON ADDLEPLOT
Now, son of a whore, do I know the gentlemen?—A dog! would have had a shilling of me before he would let me come to you!

RANGER
The rogue has been bred at Court, sure.—Get you out, sirrah.

[Exit **WAITER**.

SIR SIMON ADDLEPLOT
He has been bred at a French-house, where they are more unreasonable.

VINCENT
Here's to you, Sir Simon.

SIR SIMON ADDLEPLOT
I cannot drink, for I have a mistress within; though I would not have the people of the house to know it.

RANGER
You need not be ashamed of your mistresses, for they are commonly rich.

SIR SIMON ADDLEPLOT
And because she is rich, I would conceal her; for I never had a rich mistress yet, but one or other got her from me presently, faith and troth.

RANGER
But this is an ill place to conceal a mistress in; every waiter is an intelligencer to your rivals.

SIR SIMON ADDLEPLOT
I have a trick for that:—I'll let no waiters come into the room; I'll lay the cloth myself rather.

RANGER
But who is your mistress?

SIR SIMON ADDLEPLOT
Your servant,—your servant, Mr. Ranger.

VINCENT
Come, will you pledge me?

SIR SIMON ADDLEPLOT
No, I'll spare your wine, if you will spare me Dapperwit's company; I came for that.

VINCENT
You do us a double favour, to take him and leave the wine.

SIR SIMON ADDLEPLOT
Come, come, Dapperwit.

RANGER [Aside to **DAPPERWIT**]
Do not go, unless he will suffer us to see his mistress too.

SIR SIMON ADDLEPLOT
Come, come, man.

DAPPERWIT
Would you have me so uncivil as to leave my company?—they'll take it ill.

SIR SIMON ADDLEPLOT
I cannot find her talk without thee.—Pray, gentlemen, persuade Mr. Dapperwit to go with me.

RANGER
We will not hinder him of better company.

DAPPERWIT
Yours is too good to be left rudely.

SIR SIMON ADDLEPLOT
Nay, gentlemen, I would desire your company too, if you knew the lady.

DAPPERWIT
They know her as well as I; you say I know her not.

SIR SIMON ADDLEPLOT
You are not everybody.

RANGER
Perhaps we do know the lady, Sir Simon.

SIR SIMON ADDLEPLOT
You do not, you do not: none of you ever saw her in your lives;—but if you could be secret, and civil—

RANGER
We have drunk yet but our bottle a-piece.

SIR SIMON ADDLEPLOT
But will you be civil, Mr. Vincent?

RANGER
He dares not look a woman in the face under three bottles.

SIR SIMON ADDLEPLOT
Come along then. But can you be civil, gentlemen? will you be civil, gentlemen? pray be civil if you can, and you shall see her.

[Exit, and returns with **LADY FLIPPANT** and **MRS JOYNER**.

DAPPERWIT [Aside]
How, has he got his jilt here!

RANGER [Aside]
The widow Flippant!

VINCENT [Aside]
Is this the woman that we never saw!

LADY FLIPPANT [Aside]
Does he bring us into company!—and Dapperwit one! Though I had married the fool, I thought to have reserved the wit as well as other ladies.

SIR SIMON ADDLEPLOT
Nay, look as long as you will, madam, you will find them civil gentlemen, and good company.

LADY FLIPPANT
I am not in doubt of their civility, but yours.

MRS JOYNER [Aside to **LADY FLIPPANT**]
You'll never leave snubbing your servants! Did you not promise to use him kindly?

LADY FLIPPANT [Aside to **MRS JOYNER**]
'Tis true.—
[Aloud]
We wanted no good company, Sir Simon, as long as we had yours.

SIR SIMON ADDLEPLOT
But they wanted good company, therefore I forced 'em to accept of yours.

LADY FLIPPANT
They will not think the company good they were forced into, certainly.

SIR SIMON ADDLEPLOT
A pox! I must be using the words in fashion, though I never have any luck with 'em. Mrs. Joyner, help me off.

MRS JOYNER
I suppose, madam, he means the gentlemen wanted not inclination to your company, but confidence to desire so great an honour; therefore he forced 'em.

DAPPERWIT
What makes this bawd here? Sure, mistress, you bawds should be like the small cards, though at first you make up a pack, yet, when the play begins, you should be put out as useless.

MRS JOYNER
Well, well, gibing companion: you would have the pimps kept in only? you would so?

VINCENT
What, they are quarrelling!

RANGER
Pimp and bawd agree now-a-days like doctor and apothecary.

SIR SIMON ADDLEPLOT

Try, madam, if they are not civil gentlemen; talk with 'em, while I go lay the cloth—no waiter comes here.—
[Aside]
My mother used to tell me, I should avoid all occasions of talking before my mistress, because silence is a sign of love as well as prudence.

[Lays the cloth.

LADY FLIPPANT
Methinks you look a little yellow on't, Mr. Dapperwit. I hope you do not censure me because you find me passing away a night with this fool:—he is not a man to be jealous of, sure.

DAPPERWIT
You are not a lady to be jealous of, sure.

LADY FLIPPANT
No, certainly.—But why do you look as if you were jealous then?

DAPPERWIT
If I had met you in Whetstone's park, with a drunken foot-soldier, I should not have been jealous of you.

LADY FLIPPANT
Fy, fy! now you are jealous, certainly; for people always, when they grow jealous, grow rude:—but I can pardon it since it proceeds from love certainly.

DAPPERWIT [Aside]
I am out of all hopes to be rid of this eternal old acquaintance: when I jeer her, she thinks herself praised; now I call her whore in plain English she thinks I am jealous.

LADY FLIPPANT
Sweet Mr. Dapperwit, be not so censorious, (I speak for your sake, not my own,) for jealousy is a great torment, but my honour cannot suffer certainly.

DAPPERWIT
No, certainly; but the greatest torment I have is—your love.

LADY FLIPPANT
Alas! sweet Mr. Dapperwit, indeed love is a torment: but 'tis a sweet torment; but jealousy is a bitter torment.—I do not go about to cure you of the torment of my love.

DAPPERWIT
'Tis a sign so.

LADY FLIPPANT
Come, come, look up, man; is that a rival to contest with you?

DAPPERWIT

I will contest with no rival, not with my old rival your coachman; but they have heartily my resignation; and, to do you a favour, but myself a greater, I will help to tie the knot you are fumbling for now, betwixt your cully here and you.

LADY FLIPPANT
Go, go, I take that kind of jealousy worst of all, to suspect I would be debauched to beastly matrimony.—But who are those gentlemen, pray? are they men of fortunes, Mrs. Joyner?

MRS JOYNER
I believe so.

LADY FLIPPANT
Do you believe so, indeed?—Gentlemen—

[Advancing towards **RANGER** and **VINCENT**.

RANGER
If the civility we owe to ladies had not controlled our envy to Mr. Dapperwit, we had interrupted ere this your private conversation.

LADY FLIPPANT
Your interruption, sir, had been most civil and obliging;—for our discourse was of marriage.

RANGER
That is a subject, madam, as grateful as common.

LADY FLIPPANT
O fy, fy! are you of that opinion too? I cannot suffer any to talk of it in my company.

RANGER
Are you married then, madam?

LADY FLIPPANT
No, certainly.

RANGER
I am sure so much beauty cannot despair of it.

LADY FLIPPANT
Despair of it!—

RANGER
Only those that are married, or cannot be married, hate to hear of marriage.

LADY FLIPPANT
Yet you must know, sir, my aversion to marriage is such, that you, nor no man breathing, shall ever persuade me to it.

RANGER
Cursed be the man should do so rude a thing as to persuade you to anything against your inclination! I would not do it for the world, madam.

LADY FLIPPANT
Come, come, though you seem to be a civil gentleman, I think you no better than your neighbours. I do not know a man of you all that will not thrust a woman up into a corner, and then talk an hour to her impertinently of marriage.

RANGER
You would find me another man in a corner, I assure you, madam; for you should not have a word of marriage from me, whatsoever you might find in my actions of it; I hate talking as much as you.

LADY FLIPPANT
I hate it extremely.

RANGER
I am your man then, madam; for I find just the same fault with your sex as you do with ours:—I ne'er could have to do with woman in my life, but still she would be impertinently talking of marriage to me.

LADY FLIPPANT
Observe that, Mrs. Joyner.

DAPPERWIT
Pray, Mr. Ranger, let's go; I had rather drink with Mr. Vincent, than stay here with you; besides 'tis Park-time.

RANGER [To **DAPPERWIT**]
I come.—
[To **LADY FLIPPANT**]
Since you are a lady that hate marriage, I'll do you the service to withdraw the company; for those that hate marriage hate loss of time.

LADY FLIPPANT
Will you go then, sir? but before you go, sir, pray tell me is your aversion to marriage real?

RANGER
As real as yours.

LADY FLIPPANT [Aside]
If it were no more real than mine—

RANGER
Your servant, madam.

[Turns to go.

LADY FLIPPANT

But do you hate marriage certainly?

[Plucks him back.

RANGER
Certainly.

LADY FLIPPANT
Come, I cannot believe it: you dissemble it only because I pretend it.

RANGER
Do you but pretend it then, madam?

LADY FLIPPANT [Aside]
I shall discover myself—
[Aloud]
I mean, because I hold against it, you do the same in complaisance:—for I have heard say, cunning men think to bring the coy and untractable women to tameness as they do some mad people—by humouring their frenzies.

RANGER
I am none of those cunning men, yet have too much wit to entertain the presumption of designing upon you.

LADY FLIPPANT
'Twere no such presumption neither.

DAPPERWIT
Come away; 'sdeath! don't you see your danger?

RANGER
Those aims are for Sir Simon.—Good night, madam.

LADY FLIPPANT
Will you needs go, then?—
[To **SIR SIMON ADDLEPLOT**]
The gentlemen are a-going, Sir Simon; will you let 'em?

SIR SIMON ADDLEPLOT
Nay, madam, if you cannot keep 'em, how should I?

LADY FLIPPANT
Stay, sir; because you hate marriage, I'll sing you a new song against it.
[Sings]
A spouse I do hate,
For either she's false or she's jealous;
But give us a mate
Who nothing will ask us or tell us.

She stands on no terms,
Nor chaffers, by way of indenture,
Her love for your farms;
But takes her kind man at a venture.

If all prove not right,
Without an act, process, or warning,
From wife for a night
You may be divorced in the morning.

When parents are slaves,
Their brats cannot be any other;
Great wits and great braves
Have always a punk to their mother.

Though it be the fashion for women of quality to sing any song whatever, because the words are not distinguished, yet I should have blushed to have done it now, but for you, sir.

RANGER
The song is edifying, the voice admirable—and, once more, I am your servant, madam.

LADY FLIPPANT
What, will you go too, Mr Dapperwit?

SIR SIMON ADDLEPLOT
Pray, Mr. Dapperwit, do not you go too.

DAPPERWIT
I am engaged.

SIR SIMON ADDLEPLOT
Well, if we cannot have their company, we will not have their room: ours is a private backroom; they have paid their reckoning, let's go thither again.

LADY FLIPPANT
But pray, sweet Mr. Dapperwit, do not go. Keep him, Sir Simon.

SIR SIMON ADDLEPLOT
I cannot keep him.

[Exeunt **VINCENT**, **RANGER**, and **DAPPERWIT**.

It is impossible; (the world is so;)   One cannot keep one's friend, and mistress too.

[Exeunt.

ACT THE SECOND

SCENE I.—St. James's Park at night

Enter **RANGER**, **VINCENT**, and **DAPPERWIT**.

RANGER
Hang me, if I am not pleased extremely with this new-fashioned caterwauling, this mid-night coursing in the park.

VINCENT
A man may come after supper with his three bottles in his head, reel himself sober, without reproof from his mother, aunt, or grave relation.

RANGER
May bring his bashful wench, and not have her put out of countenance by the impudent honest women of the town.

DAPPERWIT
And a man of wit may have the better of the dumb show of well-trimmed vest or fair peruke:—no man's now is whitest.

RANGER
And now no woman's modest or proud; for her blushes are hid, and the rubies on her lips are dyed, and all sleepy and glimmering eyes have lost their attraction.

VINCENT
And now a man may carry a bottle under his arm instead of his hat;—and no observing spruce fop will miss the cravat that lies on one's shoulder, or count the pimples on one's face.

DAPPERWIT
And now the brisk repartee ruins the complaisant cringe, or wise grimace.—Something 'twas, we men of virtue always loved the night.

RANGER
O blessed season!

VINCENT
For good-fellows.

RANGER
For lovers.

DAPPERWIT
And for the Muses.

RANGER

When I was a boy I loved the night so well, I had a strong vocation to be a bellman's apprentice.

VINCENT
I, a drawer.

DAPPERWIT
And I, to attend the waits of Westminster, let me perish!

RANGER
But why do we not do the duty of this and such other places;—walk, censure, and speak ill of all we meet?

DAPPERWIT
'Tis no fault of mine, let me perish!

VINCENT
Fy, fy! satirical gentlemen, this is not your time; you cannot distinguish a friend from a fop.

DAPPERWIT
No matter, no matter; they will deserve amongst 'em the worst we can say.

RANGER
Who comes here, Dapperwit?

[**PEOPLE** walk slowly over the stage.

DAPPERWIT
By the toss of his head, training of his feet, and his elbows playing at bo-peep behind his back, it should be my Lord Easy.

RANGER
And who the woman?

DAPPERWIT
My Lord what-d'ye-call's daughter, that had a child by—

VINCENT
Dapperwit, hold your tongue.

RANGER
How! are you concerned?

VINCENT
Her brother's an honest fellow, and will drink his glass.

RANGER
Prithee, Vincent, Dapperwit did not hinder drinking to-night, though he spake against it; why, then, should you interrupt his sport?—Now, let him talk of anybody.

VINCENT
So he will,—till you cut his throat.

RANGER
Why should you on all occasions thwart him, contemn him, and maliciously look grave at his jests only?

VINCENT
Why does he always rail against my friends, then, and my best friend—a beer-glass?

RANGER
Dapperwit, be your own advocate: my game, I think, is before me there.

[Exit.

DAPPERWIT
This Ranger, I think, has all the ill qualities of all your town fops;—leaving his company for a spruce lord or a wench.

VINCENT
Nay, if you must rail at your own best friends, I may forgive you railing at mine.

[Enter **LYDIA** and **LADY FLIPPANT**.—They walk over the stage.

LYDIA [Aside]
False Ranger, shall I find thee here?

VINCENT [To **DAPPER**]
Those are women, are they not?

DAPPERWIT [Aside]
The least seems to be my Lucy, sure.

VINCENT
Faith, I think I dare speak to a woman in the dark!—let's try.

DAPPERWIT
They are persons of quality of my acquaintance;—hold!

VINCENT
Nay, if they are persons of quality of your acquaintance, I may be the bolder with 'em.

[The **LADIES** go off, they follow them.

[Re-enter **LYDIA** and **LADY FLIPPANT**.

LYDIA
I come hither to make a discovery to-night.

LADY FLIPPANT
Of my love to you, certainly; for nobody but you could have debauched me to the Park, certainly. I would not return another night, if it were to redeem my dear husband from his grave.

LYDIA
I believe you:—but to get another, widow.

LADY FLIPPANT
Another husband, another husband, foh!

LYDIA
There does not pass a night here but many a match is made.

LADY FLIPPANT
That a woman of honour should have the word match in her mouth!—but I hope, madam, the fellows do not make honourable love here, do they? I abominate honourable love, upon my honour.

LYDIA
If they should make honourable love here, I know you would prevent 'em.

[Re-enter **VINCENT** and **DAPPERWIT**.—They walk slowly towards the **LADIES**.

But here come two men will inform you what to do.

LADY FLIPPANT
Do they come?—are they men certainly?

LYDIA
Prepare for an assault, they'll put you to't.

LADY FLIPPANT
Will they put us to't certainly? I was never put to't yet. If they should put us to't, I should drop down, down, certainly.

LYDIA
I believe, truly, you would not have power to run away.

LADY FLIPPANT
Therefore I will not stay the push.—They come! they come! oh, the fellows come!

[**LADY FLIPPANT** runs away, **LYDIA** follows, and **VINCENT** and **DAPPERWIT** after them.

[Re-enter **LADY FLIPPANT** at the other side, alone.

LADY FLIPPANT
So! I am got off clear! I did not run from the men, but my companion. For all their brags, men have hardly courage to set upon us when our number is equal; now they shall see I defy 'em:—for we women

have always most courage when we are alone. But, a pox! the lazy rogues come not! or they are drunk and cannot run. Oh drink! abominable drink! instead of inflaming love, it quenches it; and for one lover t encourages, it makes a thousand impotent. Curse on all wine! even Rhenish wine and sugar—

Enter **SIR SIMON ADDLEPLOT**, *muffled in a cloak.*

But fortune will not see me want; here comes a single bully,—I wish he may stand;—
For now a-nights the jostling nymph is bolder
Than modern satyr with his cloak o'er shoulder.
Well met, sir.

She puts on her mask.

SIR SIMON ADDLEPLOT
How shall I know that, forsooth? Who are you? do you know me?

LADY FLIPPANT
Who are you? don't you know me?

SIR SIMON ADDLEPLOT
Not I, faith and troth!

LADY FLIPPANT
I am glad on't; for no man e'er liked a woman the better for having known her before.

SIR SIMON ADDLEPLOT
Ay, but then one can't be so free with a new acquaintance as with an old one; she may deny one the civility.

LADY FLIPPANT
Not till you ask her.

SIR SIMON ADDLEPLOT
But I am afraid to be denied.

LADY FLIPPANT
Let me tell you, sir, you cannot disoblige us women more than in distrusting us.

SIR SIMON ADDLEPLOT
Pish! what should one ask for, when you know one's meaning?—but shall I deal freely with you?

LADY FLIPPANT
I love, of my life, men should deal freely with me; there are so few men will deal freely with one—

SIR SIMON ADDLEPLOT
Are you not a fireship, a punk, madam?

LADY FLIPPANT

Well, sir, I love raillery.

SIR SIMON ADDLEPLOT
Faith and troth, I do not rally, I deal freely.

LADY FLIPPANT
This is the time and place for freedom, sir.

SIR SIMON ADDLEPLOT
Are you handsome?

LADY FLIPPANT
Joan's as good as my lady in the dark, certainly: but men that deal freely never ask questions, certainly.

SIR SIMON ADDLEPLOT
How then! I thought to deal freely, and put a woman to the question, had been all one.

LADY FLIPPANT
But, let me tell you, those that deal freely indeed, take a woman by—

SIR SIMON ADDLEPLOT
What, what, what, what?

LADY FLIPPANT
By the hand—and lead her aside.

SIR SIMON ADDLEPLOT
Now I understand you; come along then.

[Enter behind **MUSICIANS** with torches.

LADY FLIPPANT
What unmannerly rascals are those that bring light into the Park? 'twill not be taken well from 'em by the women, certainly.—
[Aside]
Still disappointed!

SIR SIMON ADDLEPLOT
Oh, the fiddles, the fiddles! I sent for them hither to oblige the women, not to offend 'em; for I intend to serenade the whole Park to-night. But my frolic is not without an intrigue, faith and troth: for I know the fiddles will call the whole herd of vizard masks together; and then shall I discover if a strayed mistress of mine be not amongst 'em, whom I treated to-night at the French-house; but as soon as the jilt had eat up my meat and drunk her two bottles, she ran away from me, and left me alone.

LADY FLIPPANT [Aside]
How! is it he? Addleplot!—that I could not know him by his faith and troth!

SIR SIMON ADDLEPLOT

Now I would understand her tricks; because I intend to marry her, and should be glad to know what I must trust to.

LADY FLIPPANT [Aside]
So thou shalt;—but not yet.

SIR SIMON ADDLEPLOT
Though I can give a great guess already; for if I have any intrigue or sense in me, she is as arrant a jilt as ever pulled pillow from under husband's head, faith and troth. Moreover she is bow-legged, hopper-hipped, and, betwixt pomatum and Spanish red, has a complexion like a Holland cheese, and no more teeth left than such as give a haut goût to her breath; but she is rich, faith and troth.

LADY FLIPPANT [Aside]
Oh rascal! he has heard somebody else say all this of me. But I must not discover myself, lest I should be disappointed of my revenge; for I will marry him.

[The **MUSICIANS** approaching, exit **LADY FLIPPANT**.

SIR SIMON ADDLEPLOT
What, gone!—come then, strike up, my lads.

[Enter **MEN** and **WOMEN** in vizards—a Dance, during which **SIR SIMON ADDLEPLOT**, for the most part, stands still in a cloak and vizard; but sometimes goes about peeping, and examining the Women's clothes—the Dance ended, all exeunt.

[Re-enter **LADY FLIPPANT** and **LYDIA**, after them **VINCENT** and **DAPPERWIT**.

LADY FLIPPANT [To **LYDIA**]
Nay, if you stay any longer, I must leave you again.

[Going off.

VINCENT
We have overtaken them at last again. These are they: they separate too; and that's but a challenge to us.

DAPPERWIT
Let me perish! ladies—

LYDIA
Nay, good madam, let's unite, now here's the common enemy upon us.

VINCENT
Damn me! ladies—

DAPPERWIT
Hold, a pox! you are too rough.—Let me perish! ladies—

LYDIA
Not for want of breath, gentlemen:—we'll stay rather.

DAPPERWIT
For want of your favour rather, sweet ladies.

LADY FLIPPANT [Aside]
That's Dapperwit, false villain! but he must not know I am here. If he should, I should lose his thrice agreeable company, and he would run from me as fast as from the bailiffs.
[To **LYDIA**]
What! you will not talk with 'em, I hope?

LYDIA
Yes, but I will.

LADY FLIPPANT
Then you are a Park-woman certainly, and you will take it kindly if I leave you.

LYDIA
No, you must not leave me.

LADY FLIPPANT
Then you must leave them.

LYDIA
I'll see if they are worse company than you, first.

LADY FLIPPANT
Monstrous impudence!—will you not come?

[Pulls **LYDIA**.

VINCENT
Nay, madam, I never suffer any violence to be used to a woman but what I do myself: she must stay, and you must not go.

LADY FLIPPANT
Unhand me, you rude fellow!

VINCENT
Nay, now I am sure you will stay and be kind; for coyness in a woman is as little sign of true modesty, as huffing in a man is of true courage.

DAPPERWIT
Use her gently, and speak soft things to her.

LYDIA [Aside]
Now do I guess I know my coxcomb.—

[To **DAPPERWIT**]
Sir, I am extremely glad I am fallen into the hands of a gentleman that can speak soft things; and this is so fine a night to hear soft things in;—morning, I should have said.

DAPPERWIT
It will not be morning, dear madam, till you pull off your mask.—
[Aside]
That I think was brisk.

LYDIA
Indeed, dear sir, my face would frighten back the sun.

DAPPERWIT
With glories more radiant than his own.—
[Aside]
I keep up with her, I think.

LYDIA
But why would you put me to the trouble of lighting the world, when I thought to have gone to sleep?

DAPPERWIT
You only can do it, dear madam, let me perish!

LYDIA
But why would you (of all men) practise treason against your friend Phœbus, and depose him for a mere stranger?

DAPPERWIT [Aside]
I think she knows me.

LYDIA
But he does not do you justice, I believe; and you are so positively cock-sure of your wit, you would refer to a mere stranger your plea to the bay-tree.

DAPPERWIT [Aside]
She jeers me, let me perish!

VINCENT
Dapperwit, a little of your aid; for my lady's invincibly dumb.

DAPPERWIT [Aside]
Would mine had been so too!

VINCENT
I have used as many arguments to make her speak, as are requisite to make other women hold their tongues.

DAPPERWIT

Well, I am ready to change sides.—Yet before I go, madam, since the moon consents now I should see your face, let me desire you to pull off your mask; which to a handsome lady is a favour, I'm sure.

LYDIA
Truly, sir, I must not be long in debt to you for the obligation; pray let me hear you recite some of your verses; which to a wit is a favour, I'm sure.

DAPPERWIT
Madam, it belongs to your sex to be obliged first; pull off your mask, and I'll pull out my paper.—
[Aside]
Brisk again, of my side.

LYDIA
'Twould be in vain, for you would want a candle now.

DAPPERWIT [Aside]
I dare not make use again of the lustre of her face.—
[To **LYDIA**]
I'll wait upon you home then, madam.

LYDIA
Faith, no; I believe it will not be much to our advantages to bring my face or your poetry to light: for I hope you have yet a pretty good opinion of my face, and so have I of your wit. But if you are for proving your wit, why do not you write a play?

DAPPERWIT
Because 'tis now no more reputation to write a play, than it is honour to be a knight. Your true wit despises the title of poet, as much as your true gentleman the title of knight; for as a man may be a knight and no gentleman, so a man may be a poet and no wit, let me perish!

LYDIA
Pray, sir, how are you dignified or distinguished amongst the rates of wits? and how many rates are there?

DAPPERWIT
There are as many degrees of wits as of lawyers: as there is first your solicitor, then your attorney, then your pleading-counsel, then your chamber-counsel, and then your judge; so there is first your court-wit, your coffee-wit, your poll-wit, or politic-wit, your chamber-wit, or scribble-wit, and last of all, your judge-wit, or critic.

LYDIA
But are there as many wits as lawyers? Lord, what will become of us!—What employment can they have? how are they known?

DAPPERWIT
First, your court-wit is a fashionable, insinuating, flattering, cringing, grimacing fellow—and has wit enough to solicit a suit of love; and if he fail, he has malice enough to ruin the woman with a dull lampoon:—but he rails still at the man that is absent, for you must know all wits rail; and his wit

properly lies in combing perukes, matching ribbons, and being severe, as they call it, upon other people's clothes.

LYDIA
Now, what is the coffee-wit?

DAPPERWIT
He is a lying, censorious, gossiping, quibbling wretch, and sets people together by the ears over that sober drink, coffee: he is a wit, as he is a commentator, upon the Gazette; and he rails at the pirates of Algier, the Grand Signior of Constantinople, and the Christian Grand Signior.

LYDIA
What kind of man is your poll-wit?

DAPPERWIT
He is a fidgetting, busy, dogmatical, hot-headed fop, that speaks always in sentences and proverbs, (as other in similitudes,) and he rails perpetually against the present government. His wit lies in projects and monopolies, and penning speeches for young parliament men.

LYDIA
But what is your chamber-wit, or scribble-wit?

DAPPERWIT
He is a poring, melancholy, modest sot, ashamed of the world: he searches all the records of wit, to compile a breviate of them for the use of players, printers, booksellers, and sometimes cooks, tobacco-men; he employs his railing against the ignorance of the age, and all that have more money than he.

LYDIA
Now your last.

DAPPERWIT
Your judge-wit, or critic, is all these together, and yet has the wit to be none of them: he can think, speak, write, as well as the rest, but scorns (himself a judge) to be judged by posterity: he rails at all the other classes of wits, and his wit lies in damning all but himself:—he is your true wit.

LYDIA
Then, I suspect you are of his form.

DAPPERWIT
I cannot deny it, madam.

VINCENT
Dapperwit, you have been all this time on the wrong side; for you love to talk all, and here's a lady would not have hindered you.

DAPPERWIT [Aside]
A pox! I have been talking too long indeed here; for wit is lost upon a silly weak woman, as well as courage.

VINCENT
I have used all common means to move a woman's tongue and mask; I called her ugly, old, and old acquaintance, and yet she would not disprove me:—but here comes Ranger, let him try what he can do; for, since my mistress is dogged, I'll go sleep alone.

[Exit.

[Re-enter **RANGER**.

LYDIA [Aside]
Ranger! 'tis he indeed: I am sorry he is here, but glad I discovered him before I went. Yet he must not discover me, lest I should be prevented hereafter in finding him out. False Ranger!—
[To **LADY FLIPPANT**]
Nay, if they bring fresh force upon us, madam, 'tis time to quit the field.

[Exeunt **LYDIA** and **LADY FLIPPANT**.

RANGER
What, play with your quarry till it fly from you!

DAPPERWIT
You frighten it away.

RANGER
Ha! is not one of those ladies in mourning?

DAPPERWIT
All women are so by this light.

RANGER
But you might easily discern. Don't you know her?

DAPPERWIT
No.

RANGER
Did you talk with her?

DAPPERWIT
Yes, she is one of your brisk silly baggages.

RANGER
'Tis she, 'tis she!—I was afraid I saw her before; let us follow 'em: prithee make haste.—
[Aside]
'Tis Lydia.

[Exeunt.

Re-enter, on the other side, **LYDIA** *and* **LADY FLIPPANT**—**DAPPERWIT** *and* **RANGER** *following them at a distance.*

LYDIA
They follow us yet, I fear.

LADY FLIPPANT
You do not fear it certainly; otherwise you would not have encouraged them.

LYDIA
For Heaven's sake, madam, waive your quarrel a little, and let us pass by your coach, and so on foot to your acquaintance in the old Pall-mall: for I would not be discovered by the man that came up last to us.

[*Exeunt.*

SCENE II.—Christina's Lodging

Enter **CHRISTINA** *and* **ISABEL**.

ISABEL
For Heaven's sake, undress yourself, madam! They'll not return to-night: all people have left the Park an hour ago.

CHRISTINA
What is't o'clock?

ISABEL
'Tis past one.

CHRISTINA
It cannot be!

ISABEL
I thought that time had only stolen from happy lovers:—the disconsolate have nothing to do but to tell the clock.

CHRISTINA
I can only keep account with my misfortunes.

ISABEL
I am glad they are not innumerable.

CHRISTINA
And, truly, my undergoing so often your impertinency is not the least of them.

ISABEL
I am then more glad, madam, for then they cannot be great; and it is in my power, it seems, to make you in part happy, if I could but hold this villainous tongue of mine: but then let the people of the town hold their tongues if they will, for I cannot but tell you what they say.

CHRISTINA
What do they say?

ISABEL
Faith, madam, I am afraid to tell you, now I think on't.

CHRISTINA
Is it so ill?

ISABEL
O, such base, unworthy things!

CHRISTINA
Do they say I was really Clerimont's wench, as he boasted; and that the ground of the quarrel betwixt Valentine and him was not Valentine's vindication of my honour, but Clerimont's jealousy of him?

ISABEL
Worse, worse a thousand times! such villainous things to the utter ruin of your reputation!

CHRISTINA
What are they?

ISABEL
Faith, madam, you'll be angry: 'tis the old trick of lovers to hate their informers, after they have made 'em such.

CHRISTINA
I will not be angry.

ISABEL
They say then, since Mr. Valentine's flying into France you are grown mad, have put yourself into mourning, live in a dark room, where you'll see nobody, nor take any rest day or night, but rave and talk to yourself perpetually.

CHRISTINA
Now, what else?

ISABEL
But the surest sign of your madness is, they say, because you are desperately resolved (in case my Lord Clerimont should die of his wounds) to transport yourself and fortune into France to Mr. Valentine, a man that has not a groat to return you in exchange.

CHRISTINA

All this, hitherto, is true; now to the rest.

ISABEL
Indeed, madam, I have no more to tell you. I was sorry, I'm sure, to hear so much of any lady of mine.

CHRISTINA
Insupportable insolence!

ISABEL [Aside]
This is some revenge for my want of sleep to-night.—
[Knocking at the door]
So, I hope my old second is come; 'tis seasonable relief.

[Exit.

CHRISTINA
Unhappy Valentine! couldst thou but see how soon thy absence and misfortunes have disbanded all thy friends, and turned thy slaves all renegadoes, thou sure wouldst prize my only faithful heart!

[Enter **LADY FLIPPANT**, **LYDIA**, and **ISABEL**.

LADY FLIPPANT
Hail, faithful shepherdess! but, truly, I had not kept my word with you, in coming back to-night, if it had not been for this lady, who has her intrigues too with the fellows as well as you.

LYDIA
Madam, under my Lady Flippant's protection, I am confident to beg yours; being just now pursued out of the Park by a relation of mine, by whom it imports me extremely not to be discovered:—
[Knocking at the door]
—but I fear he is now at the door.—
[To **ISABEL**, who goes out]
Let me desire you to deny me to him courageously;—for he will hardly believe he can be mistaken in me.

CHRISTINA
In such an occasion, where impudence is requisite, she will serve you as faithfully as you can wish, madam.

LADY FLIPPANT
Come, come, madam, do not upbraid her with her assurance, a qualification that only fits her for a lady's service. A fine woman of the town can be no more without a woman that can make an excuse with assurance, than she can be without a glass, certainly.

CHRISTINA
She needs no advocate.

LADY FLIPPANT

How can any one alone manage an amorous intrigue? though the birds are tame, somebody must help draw the net. If 'twere not for a woman that could make an excuse with assurance, how should we wheedle, jilt, trace, discover, countermine, undermine, and blow up the stinking fellows? which is all the pleasure I receive, or design by them; for I never admitted a man to my conversation, but for his punishment, certainly.

CHRISTINA
Nobody will doubt that, certainly.

[Re-enter **ISABEL**.

ISABEL
Madam, the gentleman will not be mistaken: he says you are here, he saw you come in; he is your relation, his name's Ranger, and is come to wait upon you home. I had much ado to keep him from coming up.

LYDIA [To **CHRISTINA**]
Madam, for Heaven's sake, help me! 'tis yet in your power; if but, while I retire into your dining-room, you will please to personate me, and own yourself for her he pursued out of the Park: you are in mourning too, and your stature so much mine it will not contradict you.

CHRISTINA
I am sorry, madam, I must dispute any command of yours. I have made a resolution to see the face of no man, till an unfortunate friend of mine, now out of the kingdom, return.

LYDIA
By that friend, and by the hopes you have to see him, let me conjure you to keep me from the sight of mine now. Dear madam, let your charity prevail over you superstition.

ISABEL
He comes, he comes, madam!

[**LYDIA** withdraws, and stands unseen at the door.

[Enter **RANGER**.

RANGER [Aside]
Ha! this is no Lydia.

CHRISTINA
What, unworthy defamer, has encouraged you to offer this insolence?

RANGER [Aside]
She is liker Lydia in her style than her face. I see I am mistaken; but to tell her I followed her for another, were an affront rather than an excuse. She's a glorious creature!

CHRISTINA

Tell me, sir, whence had you reason for this your rude pursuit of me, into my lodgings, my chamber? why should you follow me?

RANGER
Faith, madam, because you ran away from me.

CHRISTINA
That was no sign of an acquaintance.

RANGER
You'll pardon me, madam.

CHRISTINA
Then, it seems, you mistook me for another, and the night is your excuse, which blots out all distinctions. But now you are satisfied in your mistake, I hope you will seek out your woman in another place.

RANGER
Madam, I allow not the excuse you make for me. If I have offended, I will rather be condemned for my love, than pardoned for my insensibility.

LYDIA [Aside]
How's that?

CHRISTINA
What do you say?

RANGER
Though the night had been darker, my heart would not have suffered me to follow any one but you:—he has been too long acquainted with you to mistake you.

LYDIA [Aside]
What means this tenderness? he mistook me for her sure.

CHRISTINA
What says the gentleman? did you know me then, sir?

RANGER [Aside]
Not I, the devil take me! but I must on now.—
[Aloud]
Could you imagine, madam, by the innumerable crowd of your admirers, you had left any man free in the town, or ignorant of the power of your beauty?

CHRISTINA
I never saw your face before, that I remember.

RANGER
Ah, madam! you would never regard your humblest slave; I was till now a modest lover.

LYDIA [Aside]
Falsest of men!

CHRISTINA
My woman said, you came to seek a relation here, not a mistress.

RANGER
I must confess, madam, I thought you would sooner disprove my dissembled error, than admit my visit, and was resolved to see you.

LYDIA [Aside]
'Tis clear!

RANGER
Indeed, when I followed you first out of the Park, I was afraid you might have been a certain relation of mine, for your statures and habits are the same; but when you entered here, I was with joy convinced. Besides, I would not for the world have given her troublesome love so much encouragement, to have disturbed my future addresses to you; for the foolish woman does perpetually torment me to make our relation nearer; but never more in vain than since I have seen you, madam.

LYDIA [Aside]
How! shall I suffer this? 'tis clear he disappointed me to-night for her, and made me stay at home that I might not disappoint him of her company in the Park.

CHRISTINA
I am amazed! but let me tell you, sir, if the lady were here, I would satisfy her the sight of me should never frustrate her ambitious designs upon her cruel kinsman.

LYDIA [Aside]
I wish you could satisfy me.

RANGER
If she were here, she would satisfy you she were not capable of the honour to be taken for you:— though in the dark. Faith, my cousin is but a tolerable woman to a man that had not seen you.

CHRISTINA
Sure, to my plague, this is the first time you ever saw me!

RANGER
Sure, to the plague of my poor heart, 'tis not the hundredth time I have seen you! For, since the time I saw you first, you have not been at the Park, playhouse, Exchange, or other public place, but I saw you; for it was my business to watch and follow.

CHRISTINA
Pray, when did you see me last at the Park, playhouse, or Exchange?

RANGER

Some two, three days, or a week ago.

CHRISTINA
I have not been this month out of this chamber.

LYDIA [Aside]
That is to delude me.

CHRISTINA
I knew you were mistaken.

RANGER
You'll pardon a lover's memory, madam.—
[Aside]
A pox! I have hanged myself in my own line. One would think my perpetual ill-luck in lying should break me of the quality; but, like a losing gamester, I am still for pushing on, till none will trust me.

CHRISTINA
Come, sir, you run out of one error into a greater: you would excuse the rudeness of your mistake, and intrusion at this hour into my lodgings, with your gallantry to me,—more unseasonable and offensive.

RANGER
Nay, I am in love I see, for I blush and have not a word to say for myself.

CHRISTINA
But, sir, if you will needs play the gallant, pray leave my house before morning, lest you should be seen go hence, to the scandal of my honour. Rather than that should be, I'll call up the house and neighbours to bear witness I bid you begone.

RANGER
Since you take a night visit so ill, madam, I will never wait upon you again but by day. I go, that I may hope to return; and, for once, I wish you a good night without me.

CHRISTINA
Good night, for as long as I live.

[Exit **RANGER**.

LYDIA [Aside]
And good night to my love, I'm sure.

CHRISTINA
Though I have done you an inconsiderable service, I assure you, madam, you are not a little obliged to me.—
[Aside]
Pardon me, dear Valentine!

LYDIA

I know not yet whether I am more obliged than injured: when I do, I assure you, madam, I shall not be insensible of either.

CHRISTINA
I fear, madam, you are as liable to mistakes as your kinsman.

LYDIA
I fear I am more subject to 'em: it may be for want of sleep, therefore I'll go home.

CHRISTINA
My Lady Flippant, good night.

LADY FLIPPANT
Good night, or rather good morrow, faithful shepherdess.

CHRISTINA
I'll wait on you down.

LYDIA
Your coach stays yet, I hope.

LADY FLIPPANT
Certainly.

[Exeunt.

SCENE III.—The Street before Christina's Lodging

Enter **RANGER** and **DAPPERWIT**.

DAPPERWIT
I was a faithful sentinel: nobody came out, let me perish!

RANGER
No, no, I hunted upon a wrong scent; I thought I had followed a woman, but found her an angel.

DAPPERWIT
What is her name?

RANGER
That you must tell me. What very fine woman is there lives hereabouts?

DAPPERWIT
Faith, I know not any. She is, I warrant you, some fine woman of a term's standing or so in the town; such as seldom appear in public, but in their balconies, where they stand so constantly, one would think they had hired no other part of the house.

RANGER

And look like the pictures which painters expose to draw in customers;—but I must know who she is. Vincent's lodging is hard by, I'll go and inquire of him, and lie with him to-night: but if he will not let me, I'll lie with you, for my lodging is too far off.

DAPPERWIT

Then I will go before, and expect you at mine.

[*Exeunt.*

SCENE IV.—Vincent's Lodging

Enter VINCENT *and* VALENTINE *in a riding habit, as newly from a journey.*

VINCENT

Your mistress, dear Valentine, will not be more glad to see you! but my wonder is no less than my joy, that you would return ere you were informed Clerimont were out of danger. His surgeons themselves have not been assured of his recovery till within these two days.

VALENTINE

I feared my mistress, not my life. My life I could trust again with my old enemy Fortune; but no longer my mistress in the hands of my greater enemies, her relations.

VINCENT

Your fear was in the wrong place, then: for though my Lord Clerimont live, he and his relations may put you in more danger of your life than your mistress's relations can of losing her.

VALENTINE

Would any could secure me her! I would myself secure my life, for I should value it then.

VINCENT

Come, come; her relations can do you no hurt. I dare swear, if her mother should but say, "Your hat did not cock handsomely," she would never ask her blessing again.

VALENTINE

Prithee leave thy fooling, and tell me if, since my departure, she has given evidences of her love, to clear those doubts I went away with:—for as absence is the bane of common and bastard love, 'tis the vindication of that which is true and generous.

VINCENT

Nay, if you could ever doubt her love, you deserve to doubt on; for there is no punishment great enough for jealousy—but jealousy.

VALENTINE

You may remember, I told you before my flight I had quarrelled with the defamer of my mistress, but I thought I had killed my rival.

VINCENT
But pray give me now the answer which the suddenness of your flight denied me;—how could Clerimont hope to subdue her heart by the assault of her honour?

VALENTINE
Pish! it might be the stratagem of a rival to make me desist.

VINCENT
For shame! if 'twere not rather to vindicate her, than satisfy you, I would not tell you how like a Penelope she has behaved herself in your absence.

VALENTINE
Let me know.

VINCENT
Then know, the next day you went she put herself in mourning, and—

VALENTINE
That might be for Clerimont, thinking him dead, as all the world besides thought.

VINCENT
Still turning the dagger's point on yourself! hear me out. I say she put herself into mourning for you—locked herself in her chamber this month for you—shut out her barking relations for you—has not seen the sun or the face of man since she saw you—thinks and talks of nothing but you—sends to me daily to hear of you—and, and, in short, (I think,) is mad for you. All this I can swear; for I am to her so near a neighbour, and so inquisitive a friend for you—

[Enter **SERVANT**.

SERVANT
Mr. Ranger, sir, is coming up.

VINCENT
What brings him now? he comes to lie with me.

VALENTINE
Who, Ranger?

VINCENT
Yes. Pray retire a little, till I send him off:—unless you have a mind to have your arrival published to-morrow in the coffee houses.

[**VALENTINE** retires to the door behind.

[Enter **RANGER**.

RANGER
What! not yet a-bed? your man is laying you to sleep with usquebaugh or brandy; is he not so?

VINCENT
What punk will not be troubled with you to-night, therefore I am?—is it not so?

RANGER
I have been turned out of doors, indeed, just now, by a woman,—but such a woman, Vincent!

VINCENT
Yes, yes, your women are always such women!

RANGER
A neighbour of yours, and I'm sure the finest you have.

VINCENT
Prithee do not asperse my neighbourhood with your acquaintance; 'twould bring a scandal upon an alley.

RANGER
Nay, I do not know her; therefore I come to you.

VINCENT
'Twas no wonder she turned you out of doors, then; and if she had known you, 'twould have been a wonder she had let you stay. But where does she live?

RANGER
Five doors off, on the right hand.

VINCENT
Pish! pish!—

RANGER
What's the matter?

VINCENT
Does she live there, do you say?

RANGER
Yes; I observed them exactly, that my account from you might be exact. Do you know who lives there?

VINCENT
Yes, so well, that I know you are mistaken.

RANGER
Is she not a young lady scarce eighteen, of extraordinary beauty, her stature next to low, and in mourning?

VALENTINE [Aside]
What is this?

VINCENT
She is; but if you saw her, you broke in at window.

RANGER
I chased her home from the Park, indeed, taking her for another lady who had some claim to my heart, till she showed a better title to't.

VINCENT
Hah! hah! hah!

VALENTINE [Aside]
Was she at the Park, then? and have I a new rival?

VINCENT
From the Park did you follow her, do you say?—I knew you were mistaken.

RANGER
I tell you I am not.

VINCENT
If you are sure it was that house, it might be perhaps her woman stolen to the Park, unknown to her lady.

RANGER
My acquaintance does usually begin with the maid first, but now 'twas with the mistress, I assure you.

VINCENT
The mistress!—I tell you she has not been out of her doors since Valentine's flight. She is his mistress,—the great heiress, Christina.

RANGER
I tell you then again, I followed that Christina from the Park home, where I talked with her half an hour, and intend to see her to morrow again.

VALENTINE [Aside]
Would she talk with him too!

VINCENT
It cannot be.

RANGER
Christina do you call her? Faith I am sorry she is an heiress, lest it should bring the scandal of interest, and the design of lucre, upon my love.

VINCENT
No, no, her face and virtues will free you from that censure. But, however, 'tis not fairly done to rival your friend Valentine in his absence; and when he is present you know 'twill be dangerous, by my Lord Clerimont's example. Faith, if you have seen her, I would not advise you to attempt it again.

RANGER
You may be merry, sir, you are not in love; your advice I come not for, nor will I for your assistance;— Good night.

Exit.

VALENTINE
Here's your Penelope! the woman that had not seen the sun, nor face of man, since my departure! for it seems she goes out in the night, when the sun is absent, and faces are not distinguished.

VINCENT
Why! do you believe him?

VALENTINE
Should I believe you?

VINCENT
'Twere more for your interest, and you would be less deceived. If you believe him, you must doubt the chastity of all the fine women in town, and five miles about.

VALENTINE
His reports of them will little invalidate his testimony with me.

VINCENT
He spares not the innocents in bibs and aprons. I'll secure you, he has made (at best) some gross mistake concerning Christina, which to-morrow will discover; in the meantime let us go to sleep.

VALENTINE
I will not hinder you, because I cannot enjoy it myself:—
Hunger, Revenge, to sleep are petty foes,
But only Death the jealous eyes can close.

Exeunt.

ACT THE THIRD

SCENE I.—A Room in Mrs Crossbite's House

Enter **MRS JOYNER** and **MRS CROSSBITE**.

MRS JOYNER

Good morrow, gossip.

MRS CROSSBITE
Good morrow;—but why up so early, good gossip?

MRS JOYNER
My care and passionate concern for you and yours would not let me rest, in truly.

MRS CROSSBITE
For me and mine?

MRS JOYNER
You know we have known one another long; I think it be some nine-and-thirty years since you were married.

MRS CROSSBITE
Nine-and thirty years old, mistress! I'd have you to know, I am no far-born child; and if the register had not been burned in the last great fire, alas!—but my face needs no register sure; nine-and-thirty years old, said you?

MRS JOYNER
I said you had been so long married; but, indeed, you bear your years as well as any she in Pepper-alley.

MRS CROSSBITE
Nine-and-thirty, mistress!

MRS JOYNER
This it is; a woman, now-a-days, had rather you should find her faulty with a man, I warrant you, than discover her age, I warrant you.

MRS CROSSBITE
Marry, and 'tis the greatest secret far. Tell a miser he is rich, and a woman she is old,—you will get no money of him, not kindness of her. To tell me I was nine-and-thirty—(I say no more) 'twas un-neighbourly done of you, mistress.

MRS JOYNER
My memory confesses my age, it seems, as much as my face; for I thought—

MRS CROSSBITE
Pray talk nor think no more of any one's age; but say what brought you hither so early.

MRS JOYNER
How does my sweet god-daughter, poor wretch?

MRS CROSSBITE
Well, very well.

MRS JOYNER

Ah, sweet creature! Alas! alas!—I am sorry for her.

MRS CROSSBITE
Why, what has she done to deserve your sorrow, or my reprehension?

[Enter **LUCY**, and stands unseen at the door.

LUCY [Aside]
What, are they talking of me?

MRS JOYNER
In short, she was seen going into the meeting-house of the wicked, otherwise called the playhouse, hand in hand with that vile fellow Dapperwit.

MRS CROSSBITE
Mr. Dapperwit! let me tell you, if 'twere not for Master Dapperwit, we might have lived all this vacation upon green cheese, tripe, and ox cheek. If he had it, we should not want it; but, poor gentleman! it often goes hard with him,—for he's a wit.

MRS JOYNER
So, then, you are the dog to be fed, while the house is broken up! I say, beware! The sweet bits you swallow will make your daughter's belly swell, mistress; and, after all your junkets, there will be a bone for you to pick, mistress.

MRS CROSSBITE
Sure, Master Dapperwit is no such manner of man!

MRS JOYNER
He is a wit, you say; and what are wits, but contemners of matrons, seducers, or defamers of married women, and deflowerers of helpless virgins, even in the streets, upon the very bulks; affronters of midnight magistracy, and breakers of windows? in a word—

MRS CROSSBITE
But he is a little wit, a modest wit, and they do no such outrageous things as your great wits do.

MRS JOYNER
Nay, I dare say, he will not say himself he is a little wit if you ask him.

LUCY
Nay, I cannot hear this with patience.—
[Comes forward]
With your pardon, mother, you are as much mistaken as my godmother in Mr. Dapperwit; for he is as great a wit as any, and in what he speaks or writes as happy as any. I can assure you, he contemns all your tearing wits, in comparison of himself.

MRS JOYNER
Alas, poor young wretch! I cannot blame thee so much as thy mother, for thou art not thyself. His bewitching madrigals have charmed thee into some heathenish imp with a hard name.

LUCY
Nymph, you mean, godmother.

MRS JOYNER
But you, gossip, know what's what. Yesterday, as I told you, a fine old alderman of the city, seeing your daughter in so ill hands as Dapperwit's, was zealously, and in pure charity, bent upon her redemption; and has sent me to tell you, he will take her into his care and relieve your necessities, if you think good.

MRS CROSSBITE
Will he relieve all our necessities?

MRS JOYNER
All.

MRS CROSSBITE
Mine, as well as my daughter's?

MRS JOYNER
Yes.

MRS CROSSBITE
Well fare his heart!—D'ye hear, daughter, Mrs. Joyner has satisfied me clearly; Dapperwit is a vile fellow, and, in short, you must put an end to that scandalous familiarity between you.

LUCY
Leave sweet Mr. Dapperwit!—oh furious ingratitude! Was he not the man that gave me my first Farrendon gown, put me out of worsted stockings and handkerchiefs, taught me to dress, talk, and move well?

MRS CROSSBITE
He has taught you to talk indeed; but, huswife, I will not have my pleasure disputed.

MRS JOYNER
Nay, indeed, you are too tart with her, poor sweet soul.

LUCY
He taught me to rehearse, too,—would have brought me into the playhouse, where I might have had as good luck as others: I might have had good clothes, plate, jewels, and things so well about me, that my neighbours, the little gentlemen's wives of fifteen hundred or two thousand pounds a year, should have retired into the country, sick with envy of my prosperity and greatness.

MRS JOYNER
If you follow your mother's counsel, you are like to enjoy all you talk of sooner than by Dapperwit's assistance:—a poor wretch that goes on tick for the paper he writes his lampoons on, and the very ale and coffee that inspire him, as they say.

MRS CROSSBITE

am credibly informed so, indeed, Madam Joyner.

MRS JOYNER
Well, I have discharged my conscience; good morrow to you both.

[Exeunt severally.

SCENE II.—Mrs Crossbite's Dining-room

Enter **DAPPERWIT** and **RANGER**.

DAPPERWIT
This is the cabinet in which I hide my jewel; a small house, in an obscure, little, retired street, too.

RANGER
Vulgarly, an alley.

DAPPERWIT
Nay, I hide my mistress with as much care as a spark of the town does his money from his dun after a good hand at play; and nothing but you could have wrought upon me for a sight of her, let me perish.

RANGER
My obligation to you is great; do not lessen it by delays of the favour you promised.

DAPPERWIT
But do not censure my honour; for if you had not been in a desperate condition,—for as one nail must beat out another, one poison expel another, one fire draw out another, one fit of drinking cure the sickness of another,—so, the surfeit you took last night of Christina's eyes shall be cured by Lucy's this morning; or as—

RANGER
Nay, I bar more similitudes.

DAPPERWIT
What, in my mistress's lodging? that were as hard as to bar a young parson in the pulpit, the fifth of November, railing at the Church of Rome; or as hard as to put you to bed to Lucy and defend you from touching her; or as—

RANGER
Or as hard as to make you hold your tongue.—I shall not see your mistress, I see.

DAPPERWIT
Miss Lucy! Miss Lucy!—
[Knocks at the door and returns]
—The devil take me, if good men (I say no more) have not been upon their knees to me, to see her, and you at last must obtain it.

RANGER
I do not believe you.

DAPPERWIT
'Tis such as she; she is beautiful without affectation; amorous without impertinency; airy and brisk without impudence; frolic without rudeness; and, in a word, the justest creature breathing to her assignation.

RANGER
You praise her as if you had a mind to part with her; and yet you resolve, I see, to keep her to yourself.

DAPPERWIT
Keep her! poor creature, she cannot leave me; and rather than leave her, I would leave writing lampoons or sonnets almost.

RANGER
Well, I'll leave you with her then.

DAPPERWIT
What, will you go without seeing her?

RANGER
Rather than stay without seeing her.

DAPPERWIT
Yes, yes, you shall see her; but let me perish if I have not been offered a hundred guineas for a sight of her; by—I say no more.

RANGER [Aside]
I understand you now.—
[Aloud]
If the favour be to be purchased, then I'll bid all I have about me for't.

DAPPERWIT
Fy, fy, Mr. Ranger! you are pleasant, i'faith. Do you think I would sell the sight of my rarity?—like those gentlemen who hang out flags at Charing Cross, or like—

RANGER
Nay, then I'm gone again.

DAPPERWIT
What, you take it ill I refuse your money? rather than that should be, give us it; but take notice I will borrow it. Now I think on't, Lucy wants a gown and some knacks.

RANGER
Here.

DAPPERWIT
But I must pay it you again: I will not take it unless you engage your honour I shall pay it you again.

RANGER
You must pardon me; I will not engage my honour for such a trifle. Go, fetch her out.

DAPPERWIT
Well, she's a ravishing creature: such eyes and lips, Mr. Ranger!

RANGER
Prithee go.

DAPPERWIT
Such neck and breasts, Mr. Ranger!

RANGER
Again, prithee go.

DAPPERWIT
Such feet, legs, and thighs, Mr. Ranger!

RANGER
Prithee let me see 'em.

DAPPERWIT
And a mouth no bigger than your ring!—I need say no more.

RANGER
Would thou wert never to speak again!

DAPPERWIT
And then so neat, so sweet a creature in bed, that, to my knowledge, she does not change her sheets in half a year.

RANGER
I thank you for that allay to my impatience.

DAPPERWIT
Miss Lucy! Miss Lucy! Miss!—

[Knocking at the door.

RANGER
Will she not open? I am afraid my pretty miss is not stirring, and therefore will not admit us. Is she not gone her walk to Lamb's Conduit?

DAPPERWIT

Fy, fy, a quibble next your stomach in a morning! What if she should hear us? would you lose a mistress for a quibble? that's more than I could do, let me perish!—She's within, I hear her.

RANGER

But she will not hear you; she's as deaf as if you were a dun or a constable.

DAPPERWIT

Pish! give her but leave to gape, rub her eyes, and put on her day pinner; the long patch under the left eye; awaken the roses on her cheeks with some Spanish wool, and warrant her breath with some lemon-peel; the doors fly off the hinges, and she into my arms. She knows there is as much artifice to keep a victory as to gain it; and 'tis a sign she values the conquest of my heart.

RANGER

I thought her beauty had not stood in need of art.

DAPPERWIT

Beauty's a coward still without the help of art, and may have the fortune of a conquest but cannot keep it. Beauty and art can no more be asunder than love and honour.

RANGER

Or, to speak more like yourself, wit and judgment.

DAPPERWIT

Don't you hear the door wag yet?

RANGER

Not a whit.

DAPPERWIT

Miss! miss! 'tis your slave that calls. Come, all this tricking for him!—Lend me your comb, Mr. Ranger.

RANGER

No, I am to be preferred to-day, you are to set me off. You are in possession, I will not lend you arms to keep me out.

DAPPERWIT

A pox! don't let me be ungrateful; if she has smugged herself up for me, let me prune and flounce my peruke a little for her. There's ne'er a young fellow in the town but will do as much for a mere stranger in the playhouse.

RANGER

A wit's wig has the privilege of being uncombed in the very playhouse, or in the presence.

DAPPERWIT

But not in the presence of his mistress; 'tis a greater neglect of her than himself. Pray lend me your comb.

RANGER

I would not have men of wit and courage make use of every fop's mean arts to keep or gain a mistress.

DAPPERWIT
But don't you see every day, though a man have never so much wit and courage, his mistress will revolt to those fops that wear and comb perukes well. I'll break off the bargain, and will not receive you my partner.

RANGER
Therefore you see I am setting up for myself.

[Combs his peruke.

DAPPERWIT
She comes, she comes!—pray, your comb.

[Snatches **RANGER'S** comb.

[Enter **MRS CROSSBITE**.

MRS CROSSBITE
Bargain!—what, are you offering us to sale?

DAPPERWIT
A pox! is't she?—Here take your comb again, then.

[Returns the comb.

MRS CROSSBITE
Would you sell us? 'tis like you, y'fads.

DAPPERWIT
Sell thee!—where should we find a chapman? Go, prithee, mother, call out my dear Miss Lucy.

MRS CROSSBITE
Your Miss Lucy! I do not wonder you have the conscience to bargain for us behind our backs, since you have the impudence to claim a propriety in us to my face.

RANGER
How's this, Dapperwit?

DAPPERWIT
Come, come, this gentleman will not think the worse of a woman for my acquaintance with her. He has seen me bring your daughter to the lure with a chiney-orange, from one side of the playhouse to the other.

MRS CROSSBITE

I would have the gentleman and you to know my daughter is a girl of reputation, though she has been seen in your company; but is now so sensible of her past danger, that she is resolved never more to venture her pitcher to the well, as they say.

DAPPERWIT
How's that, widow? I wonder at your confidence.

MRS CROSSBITE
I wonder at your old impudence, that where you have had so frequent repulses you should provoke another, and bring your friend here to witness your disgrace.

DAPPERWIT
Hark you, widow, a little.

MRS CROSSBITE
What, have you mortgaged my daughter to that gentleman; and now would offer me a snip to join in the security!

DAPPERWIT [Aside]
She overhead me talk of a bargain;—'twas unlucky.—
[Aloud]
Your wrath is grounded upon a mistake; Miss Lucy herself shall be judge; call her out, pray.

MRS CROSSBITE
She shall not; she will not come to you.

DAPPERWIT
Till I hear it from her own mouth, I cannot believe it.

MRS CROSSBITE
You shall hear her say't through the door.

DAPPERWIT
I shall doubt it unless she say it to my face.

MRS CROSSBITE
Shall we be troubled with you no more then?

DAPPERWIT
If she command my death, I cannot disobey her.

MRS CROSSBITE
Come out, child.

[Enter **LUCY**, holding down her head.

DAPPERWIT
Your servant, dearest miss: can you have—

MRS CROSSBITE
Let me ask her.

DAPPERWIT
No, I'll ask her.

RANGER
I'll throw up cross or pile who shall ask her.

DAPPERWIT
Can you have the heart to say you will never more break a cheese-cake with me at New Spring Garden, the Neat-house, or Chelsea? never more sit in my lap at a new play? never more wear a suit of knots of my choice? and, last of all, never more pass away an afternoon with me again in the Green Garret?—do not forget the Green Garret.

LUCY
I wish I had never seen the Green Garret.—Damn the Green Garret!

DAPPERWIT
Damn the Green Garret!—You are strangely altered!

LUCY
'Tis you are altered.

DAPPERWIT
You have refused Colby's Mulberry-garden, and the French houses, for the Green Garret; and a little something in the Green Garret pleased you more than the best treat the other places could yield; and can you of a sudden quit the Green Garret?

LUCY
Since you have a design to pawn me for the rent, 'tis time to remove my goods.

DAPPERWIT
Thou art extremely mistaken.

LUCY
Besides, I have heard such strange things of you this morning.

DAPPERWIT
What things?

LUCY
I blush to speak 'em.

DAPPERWIT
I know my innocence, therefore take my charge as a favour. What have I done?

LUCY
Then know, vile wit, my mother has confessed just now thou wert false to me, to her too certain knowledge; and hast forced even her to be false to me too.

DAPPERWIT
Faults in drink, Lucy, when we are not ourselves, should not condemn us.

LUCY
And now to let me out to hire like a hackney!—I tell you my own dear mother shall bargain for me no more; there are as little as I can bargain for themselves now-a-days, as well as properer women.

MRS CROSSBITE
Whispering all this while!—Beware of his snares again: come away, child.

DAPPERWIT
Sweet, dear miss—

LUCY
Bargain for me!—you have reckoned without your hostess, as they say. Bargain for me! bargain for me!
[Exit.

DAPPERWIT
I must return, then, to treat with you.

MRS CROSSBITE
Treat me no treatings, but take a word for all. You shall no more dishonour my daughter, nor molest my lodgings, as you have done at all hours.

DAPPERWIT
Do you intend to change 'em, then, to Bridewell, or Long's powdering-tub?

MRS CROSSBITE
No, to a bailiff's house, and then you'll be so civil, I presume, as not to trouble us.

RANGER
Here, will you have my comb again, Dapperwit?

DAPPERWIT
A pox! I think women take inconstancy from me worse than from any man breathing.

MRS CROSSBITE
Pray, sir, forget me before you write your next lampoon.

[Exit.

[Enter **SIR SIMON ADDLEPLOT** in the dress of a Clerk.—**RANGER** retires to the background.

SIR SIMON ADDLEPLOT

Have I found you? have I found you in your by-walks, faith and troth? I am almost out of breath in following you. Gentlemen when they get into an alley walk so fast, as if they had more earnest business there than in the broad streets.

DAPPERWIT [Aside]
—How came this sot hither? Fortune has sent him to ease my choler.—You impudent rascal, who are you, that dare intrude thus on us?

[Strikes him.

SIR SIMON ADDLEPLOT [Softly]
Don't you know me, Dapperwit? sure you know me.

DAPPERWIT
Will thou dishonour me with thy acquaintance too? thou rascally, insolent, pen-and-ink man.

[Strikes him again.

SIR SIMON ADDLEPLOT [Softly]
Oh! oh! sure you know me! pray know me.

DAPPERWIT
By thy saucy familiarity, thou shouldst be a marker at a tennis-court, a barber, or a slave that fills coffee.

SIR SIMON ADDLEPLOT
Oh! oh!

DAPPERWIT
What art thou?

[Kicks him.

SIR SIMON ADDLEPLOT
Nay, I must not discover myself to Ranger for a kick or two. Oh, pray hold, sir: by that you will know me.

[Delivers him a letter.

DAPPERWIT
How, Sir Simon!

SIR SIMON ADDLEPLOT
Mum, mum, make no excuses, man; I would not Ranger should have known me for five hundred—kicks.

DAPPERWIT
Your disguise is so natural, I protest, it will excuse me.

SIR SIMON ADDLEPLOT
I know that, prithee make no excuses, I say. No ceremony between thee and I, man:—read the letter.

DAPPERWIT
What, you have not opened it!

SIR SIMON ADDLEPLOT
Prithee, don't be angry, the seal is a little cracked: for I could not help kissing Mrs. Martha's letter. The word is, now or never. Her father she finds will be abroad all this day, and she longs to see your friend Sir Simon Addleplot:—faith 'tis a pretty jest; while I am with her, and praising myself to her at no ordinary rate. Let thee and I alone at an intrigue.

DAPPERWIT
Tell her I will not fail to meet her at the place and time. Have a care of your charge; and manage your business like yourself, for yourself.

SIR SIMON ADDLEPLOT
I warrant you.

DAPPERWIT [Aside]
The gaining Gripe's daughter will make me support the loss of this young jilt here.

RANGER [Coming forward]
What fellow's that?

DAPPERWIT
A servant to a friend of mine.

RANGER
Methinks he something resembles our acquaintance Sir Simon; but it is no compliment to tell him so: for that knight is the most egregious coxcomb that ever played with lady's fan.

SIR SIMON ADDLEPLOT [Aside]
So! thanks to my disguise, I know my enemies!

RANGER
The most incorrigible ass, beyond the reproof of a kicking rival or a frowning mistress. But, if it be possible, thou dost use him worse than his mistress or rival can; thou dost make such a cully of him.

SIR SIMON ADDLEPLOT [Aside]
Does he think so too?

DAPPERWIT
Go, friend, go about your business.—

[Exit **SIR SIMON ADDLEPLOT**.

A pox! you would spoil all, just in the critical time of projection. He brings me here a summons from his mistress, to meet her in the evening; will you come to my wedding?

RANGER
Don't speak so loud, you'll break poor Lucy's heart. Poor creature, she cannot leave you; and, rather than leave her, you would leave writing of lampoons or sonnets—almost.

DAPPERWIT
Come, let her go, ungrateful baggage!—But now you talk of sonnets, I am no living wit if her love has not cost me two thousand couplets at least.

RANGER
But what would you give, now, for a new satire against women, ready made?—'Twould be as convenient to buy satires against women ready made, as it is to buy cravats ready tied.

DAPPERWIT
Or as—

RANGER
Hey, come away, come away, Mr., or as—

[Exeunt.

SCENE III.—A Room in Mrs Crossbite's House

Enter **Mrs. JOYNER** and **GRIPE.**

GRIPE
Peace, plenty, and pastime be within these walls!

MRS JOYNER
'Tis a small house, you see, and mean furniture; for no gallants are suffered to come hither. She might have had ere now as good lodgings as any in town; her Mortlake hangings, great glasses, cabinets, china, embroidered beds, Persia carpets, gold-plate, and the like, if she would have put herself forward. But your worship may please to make 'em remove to a place fit to receive one of your worship's quality; for this is a little scandalous, in truly.

GRIPE
No, no; I like it well enough:—I am not dainty. Besides, privacy, privacy, Mrs. Joyner! I love privacy in opposition to the wicked, who hate it.

[Looks about.

MRS JOYNER
What do you look for, sir?

GRIPE
Walls have ears; but, besides, I look for a private place to retire to, in time of need. Oh! here's one convenient.

[Turns up a hanging, and discovers the slender provisions of the family.

MRS JOYNER
But you see, poor innocent souls, to what use they put it;—not to hide gallants.

GRIPE
Temperance is the nurse of chastity.

MRS JOYNER
But your worship may please to mend their fare; and, when you come, may make them entertain you better than, you see, they do themselves.

GRIPE
No, I am not dainty, as I told you. I abominate entertainments;—no entertainments, pray, Mrs. Joyner.

MRS JOYNER [Aside]
No!

GRIPE
There can be no entertainment to me more luscious and savoury than communion with that little gentlewoman.—Will you call her out? I fast till I see her.

MRS JOYNER
But, in truly, your worship, we should have brought a bottle or two of Rhenish and some Naples biscuit, to have entertained the young gentlewoman. 'Tis the mode for lovers to treat their mistresses.

GRIPE
Modes! I tell you, Mrs. Joyner, I hate modes and forms.

MRS JOYNER
You must send for something to entertain her with.

GRIPE
Again entertaining!—we will be to each other a feast.

MRS JOYNER
I shall be ashamed, in truly, your worship.—Besides, the young gentlewoman will despise you.

GRIPE
I shall content her, I warrant you; leave it to me.

MRS JOYNER [Aside]
I am sure you will not content me, if you will not content her; 'tis as impossible for a man to love and be a miser, as to love and be wise, as they say.

GRIPE
While you talk of treats, you starve my eyes; I long to see the fair one; fetch her hither.

MRS JOYNER
I am ashamed she should find me so abominable a liar; I have so praised you to her, and, above all your virtues, your liberality; which is so great a virtue, that it often excuses youth, beauty, courage, wit, or anything.

GRIPE
Pish, pish! 'tis the virtue of fools; every fool can have it.

MRS JOYNER
And will your worship want it, then? I told her—

GRIPE
Why would you tell her anything of me? you know I am a modest man. But come, if you will have me as extravagant as the wicked, take that and fetch us a treat, as you call it.

MRS JOYNER
Upon my life a groat! what will this purchase?

GRIPE
Two black pots of ale and a cake, at the cellar.—Come, the wine has arsenic in't.

MRS JOYNER [Aside]
Well, I am mistaken, and my hopes are abused: I never knew any man so mortified a miser, that he would deny his lechery anything; I must be even with thee then another way.

[Exit.

GRIPE
These useful old women are more exorbitant and craving in their desires than the young ones in theirs. These prodigals in white perukes spoil 'em both; and that's the reason, when the squires come under my clutches, I make 'em pay for their folly and mine, and 'tis but conscience:—oh, here comes the fair one at last!

[Re-enter **MRS JOYNER** leading in **LUCY**, who hangs backwards as she enters.

LUCY
Oh Lord, there's a man, godmother!

MRS JOYNER
Come in, child, thou art so bashful—

LUCY
My mother is from home too, I dare not.

MRS JOYNER
If she were here, she'd teach you better manners.

LUCY
I'm afraid she'd be angry.

MRS JOYNER
To see you so much an ass.—Come along, I say.

GRIPE
Nay, speak to her gently; if you won't, I will.

LUCY
Thank you, sir.

GRIPE
Pretty innocent! there is, I see, one left of her age; what hap have I! Sweet little gentlewoman, come sit down by me.

LUCY
I am better bred, I hope, sir.

GRIPE
You must sit down by me.

LUCY
I'd rather stand, if you please.

GRIPE
To please me, you must sit, sweetest.

LUCY
Not before my godmother, sure.

GRIPE
Wonderment of innocence!

MRS JOYNER
A poor bashful girl, sir: I'm sorry she is not better taught.

GRIPE
I am glad she is not taught; I'll teach her myself.

LUCY
Are you a dancing-master then, sir? But if I should be dull, and not move as you would have me, you would not beat me, sir, I hope?

GRIPE
Beat thee, honeysuckle! I'll use thee thus, and thus, and thus.
[Kisses her]
Ah, Mrs. Joyner, prithee go fetch our treat now.

MRS JOYNER
A treat of a groat! I will not wag.

GRIPE
Why don't you go? Here, take more money, and fetch what you will; take here, half-a-crown.

MRS JOYNER
What will half-a-crown do?

GRIPE
Take a crown then, an angel, a piece;—begone!

MRS JOYNER
A treat only will not serve my turn; I must buy the poor wretch there some toys.

GRIPE
What toys? what? speak quickly.

MRS JOYNER
Pendants, necklaces, fans, ribbons, points, laces, stockings, gloves—

GRIPE
Hold, hold! before it comes to a gown.

MRS JOYNER
Well remembered, sir; indeed she wants a gown, for she has but that one to her back. For your own sake you should give her a new gown, for variety of dresses rouses desire, and makes an old mistress seem every day a new one.

GRIPE
For that reason she shall have no new gown; for I am naturally constant, and as I am still the same, I love she should be still the same. But here, take half a piece for the other things.

MRS JOYNER
Half a piece!—

GRIPE
Prithee, begone!—take t'other piece then—two pieces—three pieces—five! here, 'tis all I have.

MRS JOYNER
I must have the broad-seal ring too, or I stir not.

GRIPE
Insatiable woman! will you have that too! Prithee spare me that, 'twas my grandfather's.

MRS JOYNER [Aside]
That's false, he had ne'er a coat.—So! now I go; this is but a violent fit, and will not hold.

LUCY
Oh! whither do you go, godmother? will you leave me alone?

MRS JOYNER
The gentleman will not hurt you; you may venture yourself with him alone.

LUCY
I think I may, godmother.—

[Exit **MRS JOYNER**.

What! will you lock me in, sir? don't lock me in, sir.

[**GRIPE**, fumbling at the door, locks it.

GRIPE
'Tis a private lesson, I must teach you, fair.

LUCY
I don't see your fiddle, sir; where is your little kit?

GRIPE
I'll show it thee presently, sweetest.—
[Sets a chair against the door]
—Necessity, mother of invention!—Come, my dearest.

[Takes her in his arms.

LUCY
What do you mean, sir? don't hurt me, sir, will you—Oh! oh! you will kill me! Murder! murder!—Oh! oh!—help! help! oh!

[The door is broken open; enter **MRS CROSSBITE**, and her **LANDLORD**, and his **'PRENTICE**, in aprons.

MRS CROSSBITE
What, murder my daughter, villain!

LUCY
I wish he had murdered me.—Oh! oh!

MRS CROSSBITE
What has he done?

LUCY
Why would you go out, and leave me alone? unfortunate woman that I am!

GRIPE [Aside]

How now, what will this end in?

MRS CROSSBITE
Who brought him in?

LUCY
That witch, that treacherous false woman, my godmother, who has betrayed me, sold me to his lust.—Oh! oh!—

MRS CROSSBITE
Have you ravished my daughter, then, you old goat? ravished my daughter!—ravished my daughter! speak, villain.

GRIPE
By yea and by nay, no such matter.

MRS CROSSBITE
A canting rogue, too! Take notice, landlord, he has ravished my daughter, you see her all in tears and distraction; and see there the wicked engine of the filthy execution.—

[Pointing to the chair.

—Jeremy, call up the neighbours, and the constable,—False villain! thou shalt die for it.

GRIPE
Hold! hold!—
[Aside]
—Nay, I am caught.

MRS CROSSBITE
Go, go, make haste—

LUCY
Oh! oh!—

MRS CROSSBITE
Poor wretch!—Go quickly.

GRIPE
Hold! hold!—Thou young spawn of the old serpent! wicked, as I thought thee innocent! wilt thou say I would have ravished thee?

LUCY
I will swear you did ravish me.

GRIPE
I thought so, treacherous Eve!—then I am gone, I must shift as well as I can.

LUCY
Oh! oh!—

MRS CROSSBITE
Will none of you call up the neighbours, and the authority of the alley?

GRIPE
Hold, I'll give you twenty mark among you to let me go.

MRS CROSSBITE
Villain! nothing shall buy thy life.

LANDLORD
But stay, Mrs. Crossbite, let me talk with you.

LUCY
Oh! oh!—

LANDLORD
Come, sir, I am your friend:—in a word, I have appeased her, and she shall be contented with a little sum.

GRIPE
What is it? what is it?

LANDLORD
But five hundred pounds.

GRIPE
But five hundred pounds!—hang me then, hang me rather.

LANDLORD
You will say I have been your friend.

'PRENTICE
The constable and neighbours are a-coming.

GRIPE
How, how; will you not take a hundred? pray use conscience in your ways.

[Kneels to **MRS CROSSBITE**.

MRS CROSSBITE
I scorn your money! I will not take a thousand.

GRIPE [Aside]
My enemies are many, and I shall be a scandal to the faithful, as a laughing-stock to the wicked.—[Aloud]

Go, prepare your engines for my persecution; I'll give you the best security I can.

LANDLORD
The instruments are drawing in the other room, if you please to go thither.

MRS CROSSBITE
Indeed, now I consider, a portion will do my daughter more good than his death. That would but publish her shame; money will cover it—probatum est, as they say. Let me tell you, sir, 'tis a charitable thing to give a young maid a portion.

Exeunt.

SCENE IV.—Lydia's Lodging

Enter **LYDIA** *and* **LADY FLIPPANT**, *attended by* **LEONORE**.

LYDIA
'Tis as hard for a woman to conceal her indignation from her apostate lover, as to conceal her love from her faithful servant.

LADY FLIPPANT
Or almost as hard as it is for the prating fellows now-a-days to conceal the favours of obliging ladies.

LYDIA
If Ranger should come up, (I saw him just now in the street,) the discovery of my anger to him now would be as mean as the discovery of my love to him before.

LADY FLIPPANT
Though I did so mean a thing as to love a fellow, I would not do so mean a thing as to confess it, certainly, by my trouble to part with him. If I confessed love, it should be before they left me.

LYDIA
So you would deserve to be left, before you were. But could you ever do so mean a thing as to confess love to any?

LADY FLIPPANT
Yes; but I never did so mean a thing as really to love any.

LYDIA
You had once a husband.

LADY FLIPPANT
Fy! madam, do you think me so ill bred as to love a husband?

LYDIA
You had a widow's heart, before you were a widow, I see.

LADY FLIPPANT
I should rather make an adventure of my honour with a gallant for a gown, a new coach, a necklace, than clap my husband's cheeks for them, or sit in his lap. I should be as ashamed to be caught in such a posture with a husband, as a brisk well-bred spark of the town would be to be caught on his knees at prayers—unless to his mistress.

[Enter **RANGER** and **DAPPERWIT**.

LYDIA
Mr. Ranger, 'twas obligingly done of you.

RANGER
Indeed, cousin, I had kept my promise with you last night, but this gentleman knows—

LYDIA
You mistake me; but you shall not lessen any favour you do to me. You are going to excuse your not coming to me last night, when I take it as a particular obligation, that though you threatened me with a visit, upon consideration you were so civil as not to trouble me.

DAPPERWIT [Aside]
This is an unlucky morning with me! here's my eternal persecution, the widow Flippant.

LADY FLIPPANT
What, Mr. Dapperwit!

[**DAPPERWIT** retires to the back of the stage, followed by **LADY FLIPPANT**.

RANGER
Indeed, cousin, besides my business, another cause I did not wait on you was, my apprehension you were gone to the Park, notwithstanding your promise to the contrary.

LYDIA
Therefore, you went to the Park to visit me there, notwithstanding your promise to the contrary?

RANGER
Who, I at the Park! when I had promised to wait upon you at your lodging! But were you at the Park, madam?

LYDIA
Who, I at the Park! when I had promised to wait for you at home! I was no more at the Park than you were. Were you at the Park?

RANGER
The Park had been a dismal desert to me, notwithstanding all the good company in it, if I had wanted yours.

LYDIA [Aside]

Because it has been the constant endeavour of men to keep women ignorant, they think us so; but 'tis that increases our inquisitiveness, and makes us know them ignorant as false. He is as impudent a dissembler as the widow Flippant, who is making her importunate addresses in vain, for aught I see.

[LADY FLIPPANT comes forward, driving DAPPERWIT from one side of the stage to the other.

LADY FLIPPANT
Dear Mr. Dapperwit! merciful Mr. Dapperwit!

DAPPERWIT
Unmerciful Lady Flippant!

LADY FLIPPANT
Will you be satisfied?

DAPPERWIT
Won't you be satisfied?

LADY FLIPPANT
That a wit should be jealous; that a wit should be jealous! there's never a brisk young fellow in the town, though no wit, Heaven knows, but thinks too well of himself, to think ill of his wife or mistress. Now, that a wit should lessen his opinion of himself;—for shame!

DAPPERWIT [Softly, apart to RANGER]
I promised to bring you off, but I find it enough to shift for myself—.

LYDIA
What! out of breath, madam!

LADY FLIPPANT
I have been defending our cause, madam; I have beat him out of the pit. I do so mumble these prating, censorious fellows they call wits, when I meet with them.

DAPPERWIT
Her ladyship, indeed, is the only thing in petticoats I dread. 'Twas well for me there was company in the room; for I dare no more venture myself with her alone, than a cully that has been bit dares venture himself in a tavern with an old rook.

LADY FLIPPANT
I am the revenger of our sex, certainly.

DAPPERWIT
And the most insatiable one I ever knew, madam; I dare not stand your fury longer.—Mr. Ranger, I will go before and make a new appointment with your friends that expect you at dinner at the French-house; 'tis fit business still wait on love.

RANGER

Do so—but now I think on't, Sir Thomas goes out of town this afternoon, and I shall not see him here again these three months.

LYDIA
Nay, pray take him with you, sir.

LADY FLIPPANT
No, sir, you shall not take the gentleman from his mistress.—
[Aside to **DAPPERWIT**]
Do not go yet, sweet Mr. Dapperwit.

LYDIA
Take him with you, sir; I suppose his business may be there to borrow or win money, and I ought not to be his hindrance: for when he has none, he has his desperate designs upon that little I have;—for want of money makes as devout lovers as Christians.

DAPPERWIT
I hope, madam, he offers you no less security than his liberty.

LYDIA
His liberty is as poor a pawn to take up money on as honour. He is like the desperate bankrupts of this age, who, if they can get people's fortunes into their hands, care not though they spend them in jail all their lives.

LADY FLIPPANT
And the poor crediting ladies, when they have parted with their money, must be contented with a pitiful composition, or starve, for all them.

RANGER
But widows are commonly so wise as to be sure their men are solvable before they trust 'em.

LADY FLIPPANT
Can you blame 'em! I declare I will trust no man. Pray, do not take it ill, gentlemen: quacks in their bills, and poets in the titles of their plays, do not more disappoint us, than gallants with their promises; but I trust none.

DAPPERWIT
Nay, she's a very Jew in that particular. To my knowledge, she'll know her man, over and over again, before she trust him.

RANGER
Well, my dearest cousin, good-morrow. When I stay from you so long again, blame me to purpose, and be extremely angry; for nothing can make me amends for the loss of your company, but your reprehension of my absence. I'll take such a chiding as kindly as Russian wives do beating.

LYDIA
If you were my husband, I could not take your absence more kindly than I do.

RANGER
And if you were my wife, I would trust you as much out of my sight as I could, to show my opinion of your virtue.

LADY FLIPPANT
A well-bred gentleman, I warrant.—Will you go then, cruel Mr. Dapperwit?

[Exeunt **RANGER** and **DAPPERWIT**, followed by **LADY FLIPPANT**.

LYDIA
Have I not dissembled well, Leonore?

LEONORE
But, madam, to what purpose? why do you not put him to his trial, and see what he can say for himself?

LYDIA
I am afraid lest my proofs, and his guilt, should make him desperate, and so contemn that pardon which he could not hope for.

LEONORE
'Tis unjust to condemn him before you hear him.

LYDIA
I will reprieve him till I have more evidence.

LEONORE
How will you get it?

LYDIA
I will write him a letter in Christina's name, desiring to meet him; when I shall soon discover if his love to her be of a longer standing than since last night; and if it be not, I will not longer trust him with the vanity to think she gave him the occasion to follow her home from the Park; so will at once disabuse him and myself.

LEONORE
What care the jealous take in making sure of ills which they, but in imagination, cannot undergo!

LYDIA
Misfortunes are least dreadful when most near:
'Tis less to undergo the ill, than fear.

[Exeunt.

ACT THE FOURTH

SCENE I.—A Room in Gripe's House

Enter **Mrs. JOYNER** and **GRIPE**, the latter in a blue gown and nightcap.

MRS JOYNER
What, not well, your worship! This it is, you will be laying out yourself beyond your strength. You have taken a surfeit of the little gentlewoman, I find. Indeed you should not have been so immoderate in your embraces; your worship is something in years, in truly.

GRIPE
Graceless, perfidious woman! what makest thou here? art thou not afraid to be used like an informer, since thou hast made me pay thee for betraying me?

MRS JOYNER
Betray your worship! what do you mean? I an informer! I scorn your words!

GRIPE
Woman, I say again, thou art as treacherous as an informer, and more unreasonable; for he lets us have something for our money before he disturb us.

MRS JOYNER
Your money, I'm sure, was laid out faithfully; and I went away because I would not disturb you.

GRIPE
I had not grudged you the money I gave you:—but the five hundred pounds! the five hundred pounds! Inconscionable, false woman, the five hundred pounds!—You cheated, trepanned, robbed me, of the five hundred pounds!

MRS JOYNER
I cheat you! I rob you!—well, remember what you say, you shall answer it before Mr. Doublecap and the best of—

GRIPE
Oh, impudent woman, speak softly!

MRS JOYNER
I will not speak softly; for innocence is loud as well as barefaced. Is this your return, after you have made me a mere drudge to your filthy lusts?

GRIPE
Speak softly; my sister, daughter, and servants, will hear.

MRS JOYNER
I would have witnesses, to take notice that you blast my good name, which was as white as a tulip, and as sweet as the head of your cane, before you wrought me to the carrying on the work of your fleshly carnal seekings.

GRIPE
Softly! softly! they are coming in.

[Enter **LADY FLIPPANT** and **MRS MARTHA**.

LADY FLIPPANT
What's the matter, brother?

GRIPE
Nothing, nothing, sister, only the godly woman is fallen into a fit of zeal against the enormous transgressions of the age. Go! go! you do not love to hear vanity reproved; pray begone!

MRS JOYNER
Pray stay, madam, that you may know—

GRIPE [Aside to **MRS JOYNER**]
Hold! hold! here are five guineas for thee,—pray say nothing.—
[Aloud]
Sister, pray begone, I say.—

[Exeunt **LADY FLIPPANT** and **MRS MARTHA**.

Would you prejudice your own reputation to injure mine?

MRS JOYNER
Would you prejudice your own soul to wrong my repute, in truly?

[Pretends to weep.

GRIPE
Pray have me in excuse. Indeed, I thought you had a share of the five hundred pounds, because you took away my seal-ring; which they made me send, together with a note to my cash-keeper for five hundred pounds. Besides, I thought none but you knew it was my wonted token to send for money by.

MRS JOYNER
'Tis unlucky I should forget it, and leave it on the table!—But oh the harlotry! did she make that use of it then? 'twas no wonder you did not stay till I came back.

GRIPE
I stayed till the money released me.

MRS JOYNER
Have they the money, then? five hundred pounds!

GRIPE
Too certain.

MRS JOYNER
They told me not a word of it; and have you no way to retrieve it?

GRIPE
Not any.

MRS JOYNER [Aside]
I am glad of it.—
[Aloud]
Is there no law but against saints?

GRIPE
I will not for five hundred pounds publish my transgression myself, lest I should be thought to glory in't: though, I must confess, 'twould tempt a man to conform to public praying and sinning, since 'tis so chargeable to pray and sin in private.

MRS JOYNER
But are you resolved to give off a loser?

GRIPE
How shall I help it?

MRS JOYNER
Nay, I'll see you shall have what the young jade has, for your money; I'll make 'em use some conscience, however.—Take a man's money for nothing!

GRIPE
Thou sayest honestly, indeed. And shall I have my pennyworths out of the little gentlewoman for all this?

MRS JOYNER
I'll be engaged body for body for her, and you shall take the forfeiture on me else.

GRIPE
No, no, I'll rather take your word, Mrs. Joyner.

MRS JOYNER
Go in and dress yourself smug, and leave the rest to me.

GRIPE
No man breathing would give-off a loser, as she says.

[Exeunt.

SCENE II.—Another Room in the same

SIR SIMON ADDLEPLOT discovered sitting at a desk writing as a Clerk, **LADY FLIPPANT** jogging him.

SIR SIMON ADDLEPLOT

'Tis a lord's mortgage, and therefore requires the more haste:—pray do not jog me, madam.

LADY FLIPPANT [Aside]
Dull rascal!

SIR SIMON ADDLEPLOT
They cannot stay for money as other folks. If you will not let me make an end on't, I shall lose my expedition-fee.

LADY FLIPPANT [Aside]
There are some clerks would have understood me before this.

SIR SIMON ADDLEPLOT
Nay, pray be quiet, madam; if you squeeze me so to the wall, I cannot write.

LADY FLIPPANT [Aside]
'Tis much for the honour of the gentlemen of this age, that we persons of quality are forced to descend to the importuning of a clerk, a butler, coachman, or footman; while the rogues are as dull of apprehension, too, as an unfledged country squire amongst his mother's maids!

[Jogs him again.

SIR SIMON ADDLEPLOT
Again! Let me tell you, madam, familiarity breeds contempt: you'll never leave till you have made me saucy.

LADY FLIPPANT
I would I could see that.

SIR SIMON ADDLEPLOT
I vow and swear then, get you gone! or I'll add a black patch or two to those on your face.—
[Aside]
I shall have no time to get Mrs. Martha out, for her.

LADY FLIPPANT
Will you, sir, will you!

[Jogs him again.

SIR SIMON ADDLEPLOT [Aside]
I must have a plot for her, she is a coy woman.—
[Aloud]
I vow and swear if you pass this crevice, I'll kiss you in plain English.

LADY FLIPPANT
I would I could see that!—do you defy me!

[Steps to him—he kisses her.

SIR SIMON ADDLEPLOT [Aside]
How's this! I vow and swear, she kisses as tamely as Mrs. Ticklish, and with her mouth open too.

LADY FLIPPANT
I thought you would have been ashamed to have done so to your master's own sister!

SIR SIMON ADDLEPLOT
I hope you'll be quiet now, madam?

LADY FLIPPANT
Nay, I'll be revenged of you sure.

SIR SIMON ADDLEPLOT
If you come again, I shall do more to you than that.—
[Aside]
I'll pursue my plot and try if she be honest.

LADY FLIPPANT
You do more to me than that! nay, if you'll do more to me than that—

[She throws down his ink and runs out, he following her.

[Enter **MRS JOYNER**.

MRS JOYNER
I must visit my young clients in the meantime.

[Re-enter **SIR SIMON ADDLEPLOT**, holding up his hands.

What's the matter, Sir Simon?

SIR SIMON ADDLEPLOT
Lord! who would have thought it?

MRS JOYNER
What ails you, Sir Simon?

SIR SIMON ADDLEPLOT
I have made such a discovery, Mrs. Joyner!

MRS JOYNER
What is't?

SIR SIMON ADDLEPLOT
Such a one that makes me at once glad and sorry; I am sorry my Lady Flippant is naught, but I'm glad I know it:—thanks still to my disguise.

MRS JOYNER
Fy! fy!

SIR SIMON ADDLEPLOT
Nay, this hand can tell—

MRS JOYNER
But how?

SIR SIMON ADDLEPLOT
She threw down my ink-glass, and ran away into the next room; I followed her, and, in revenge, threw her down upon the bed:—but, in short, all that I could do to her would not make her squeak.

MRS JOYNER
She was out of breath, man, she was out of breath.

SIR SIMON ADDLEPLOT
Ah, Mrs. Joyner, say no more, say no more of that!

[Re-enter **LADY FLIPPANT**.

LADY FLIPPANT
You rude, unmannerly rascal!

MRS JOYNER
You see she complains now.

SIR SIMON ADDLEPLOT [Aside to **MRS JOYNER**]
I know why, Mrs. Joyner, I know why.

LADY FLIPPANT
I'll have you turned out of the house; you are not fit for my brother's service.

SIR SIMON ADDLEPLOT [Aside]
Not for yours, you mean, madam.

LADY FLIPPANT
I'll go and acquaint my brother—

MRS JOYNER [Aside to **LADY FLIPPANT**]
Hold, hold, madam, speak not so loud:—'tis Sir Simon Addleplot, your lover, who has taken this disguise on purpose to be near you, and to watch and supplant his rival.

LADY FLIPPANT [Aside to **MRS JOYNER**]
What a beast was I, I could not discover it! you have undone me! why would you not tell me sooner of it?

MRS JOYNER

I thought he had been discernible enough.

LADY FLIPPANT
I protest, I knew him not; for I must confess to you, my eyes are none of the best since I have used the last new wash of mercury-water.—What will he think of me!

MRS JOYNER
Let me alone with him.—
[To **SIR SIMON ADDLEPLOT**]
Come, come, did you think you could disguise yourself from my lady's knowledge? she knew you, man, or else you had ne'er had those liberties. Alas, poor lady, she cannot resist you!

LADY FLIPPANT
'Tis my weakness.

SIR SIMON ADDLEPLOT
How's this!—but here comes my master.

[Enter **GRIPE** and **MRS MARTHA**.

GRIPE
Come, Mrs. Joyner, are you ready to go?

MRS JOYNER
I am ever ready when your worship commands.

LADY FLIPPANT
Brother, if you go to t'other end of the town, you'll set me down near the playhouse?

GRIPE
The playhouse! do you think I will be seen near the playhouse?

LADY FLIPPANT
You shall set me down in Lincoln's-inn-fields, then? for I have earnest business there.—
[Apart to **SIR SIMON ADDLEPLOT**]
When I come home again, I'll laugh at you soundly, Sir Simon.

SIR SIMON ADDLEPLOT [Aside]
Has Joyner betrayed me then! 'tis time to look to my hits.

GRIPE
Martha, be sure you stay within now. If you go out, you shall never come into my doors again.

MRS MARTHA
No, I will not, sir; I'll ne'er come into your doors again, if once I should go out.

GRIPE
'Tis well said, girl.

[*Exeunt* GRIPE, MRS JOYNER, *and* LADY FLIPPANT.

SIR SIMON ADDLEPLOT
Twas prettily said: I understand you, they are dull, and have no intrigue in 'em. But dear sweet Mrs. Martha, 'tis time we were gone; you have stole away your scarfs and hood from your maid, I hope?

MRS MARTHA
Nay, I am ready, but—

SIR SIMON ADDLEPLOT
Come, come, Sir Simon Addleplot, poor gentleman, is an impatient man, to my knowledge.

MRS MARTHA
Well, my venture is great, I'm sure, for a man I know not. But pray, Jonas, do not deceive me; is he so fine a gentleman, as you say he is?

SIR SIMON ADDLEPLOT
Pish! pish! he is the—gentleman of the town, faith and troth.

MRS MARTHA
But may I take your word, Jonas?

SIR SIMON ADDLEPLOT
Tis not my word, 'tis the word of all the town.

MRS MARTHA
Excuse me, Jonas, for that:—I never heard any speak well of him but Mr. Dapperwit and you.

SIR SIMON ADDLEPLOT
That's because he has been a rival to all men, and a gallant to all ladies. Rivals and deserted mistresses never speak well of a man.

MRS MARTHA
Has he been so general in his amours? his kindness is not to be valued then.

SIR SIMON ADDLEPLOT
The more by you; because 'tis for you he deserts all the rest, faith and troth.

MRS MARTHA
You plead better for him than he could for himself, I believe; for, indeed, they say he is no better than an idiot.

SIR SIMON ADDLEPLOT
Then, believe me, madam—for nobody knows him better than I—he has as much wit, courage, and as good a mien to the full, as I have.—He an idiot!

MRS MARTHA

The common gull; so perspicuous a fop, the women find him out:—for none of 'em will marry him.

SIR SIMON ADDLEPLOT
You may see, now, how he and you are abused. For that he is not married, is a sign of his wit; and for being perspicuous, 'tis false; he is as mysterious as a new parliament-man, or a young statesman newly taken from a coffee-house or tennis-court.

MRS MARTHA
But is it a sign of his wit because he is not married?

SIR SIMON ADDLEPLOT
Yes, yes; your women of the town ravish your fops: there's not one about the town unmarried that has anything.

MRS MARTHA
It may be then he has spent his estate.

SIR SIMON ADDLEPLOT [Aside]
How unluckily guessed!—
[Aloud]
If he had, he has a head can retrieve it again.

MRS MARTHA
Besides, they say he has the modish distemper.

SIR SIMON ADDLEPLOT
He can cure it with the best French chirurgeon in town.

MRS MARTHA
Has his practice on himself been so much?

SIR SIMON ADDLEPLOT
Come, come.—
Fame, like deserted jilt, does still belie men;
Who doubts her man, must be advised by Hymen;
For he knows best of any how to try men.

[Exeunt.

SCENE III.—The old Pall Mall

Enter **RANGER** and **DAPPERWIT**.

RANGER
Now the Lucys have renounced us, hey for the Christinas! She cannot use me worse than your honourable mistress did you.

DAPPERWIT
A pox! some young heir or another has promised her marriage. There are so many fools in the world, 'tis impossible for a man of wit to keep his wench from being a lady, let me perish!

RANGER
But have you no other acquaintance that sticks to her vocation, in spite of temptations of honour or filthy lucre? I declare, I make honourable love merely out of necessity, as your rooks play on the square rather than not play at all.

[Enter **LEONORE** masked, with a letter in her hand.

DAPPERWIT
Come, the devil will not lose a gamester: here's ready money for you, push freely.

RANGER [To **LEONORE**]
Thou art as well met as if by assignation.

LEONORE
And you are as well met as if you were the man I looked for.

RANGER
Kind rogue!

LEONORE
Sweet sir!

RANGER
Come, I am thy prisoner, (without more words,) show but thy warrant.

[Goes to pull off her mask.

LEONORE
You mistake, sir; here is my pass.

[Gives him the letter.

RANGER
A letter! and directed to me!
[Reads]
"I cannot put up the injuries and affronts you did me last night;"—a challenge, upon my life! and by such a messenger!—"therefore conjure you by your honour, at eight o'clock precisely, this evening, to send your man to St. James's gate, to wait for me with a chair, to conduct me to what place you shall think most fit, for the giving of satisfaction to the injured—Christina."

Christina! I am amazed! What is it o'clock, Dapperwit?

DAPPERWIT

It wants not half an hour of eight.

RANGER [To **LEONORE**]
Go then back, my pretty herald, and tell my fair enemy the service she designs my man is only fit for my friend here; whose faith and honour she may be secure of. He shall immediately go wait for her at St James's gate, whilst I go to prepare a place for our rencounter, and myself to die at her feet.

[Exit **LEONORE**.

Dapperwit, dear Dapperwit.

DAPPERWIT
What lucky surprisal's this?

RANGER
Prithee ask no questions, till I have more leisure and less astonishment. I know you will not deny to be an instrument in my happiness.

DAPPERWIT
No, let me perish! I take as much pleasure to bring lovers together as an old woman; or as a bankrupt gamester loves to look on, though he has no advantage by the play; or as a bully that fights not himself, yet takes pleasure to set people together by the ears, or as—

RANGER
'Sdeath! is this a time for similitudes?

DAPPERWIT
You have made me miscarry of a good thought now, let me perish!

RANGER
Go presently to St. James's gate, where you are to expect the coming of a lady ('tis Christina), accompanied by that woman you saw e'en now. She will permit you to put her into a chair, and then conduct her to my lodging; while I go before to remove some spies, and prepare it for her reception.

DAPPERWIT
Your lodging? had you not better carry her to Vincent's? 'tis hard by; and there a vizard mask has as free egress and regress as at the playhouse.

RANGER
Faith, though it be not very prudent, yet she shall come thither in my vindication; for he would not believe I had seen her last night.

DAPPERWIT
To have a fine woman, and not tell on't as you say, Mr. Ranger—

RANGER
Go, and bring her to Vincent's lodging; there I'll expect you.

[Exeunt severally.

SCENE IV.—The Street before Vincent's Lodging

Enter **CHRISTINA** and **ISABEL**.

ISABEL
This is the door, madam; here Mr. Vincent lodges.

CHRISTINA
'Tis no matter, we will pass it by; lest the people of our lodgings should watch us. But if he should not be here now!

ISABEL
Who, Mr. Valentine, madam? I warrant you my intelligencer dares not fail me.

CHRISTINA
Did he come last night, said he?

ISABEL
Last night late.

CHRISTINA
And not see me yet! nay, not send to me!—'tis false, he is not come,—I wish he were not. I know not which I should take more unkindly from him, exposing his life to his revengeful enemies, or being almost four-and-twenty hours so near me, and not let me know't.

ISABEL
A lover's dangers are the only secrets kept from his mistress; he came not to you because he would not purchase his happiness with your fear and apprehensions.

CHRISTINA
Nay, he is come, I see, since you are come about again of his side.

ISABEL
Will you go in, madam, and disprove me, if you can? 'tis better than standing in the street.

CHRISTINA
We'll go a little further first, and return.

[Exeunt.

SCENE V.—Vincent's Lodging

Enter **VINCENT** and **VALENTINE**.

VINCENT
I told you I had sent my man to Christina's this morning, to inquire of her maid, (who seldom denies him a secret,) if her lady had been at the Park last night; which she peremptorily answered to the contrary, and assured him she had not stirred out since your departure.

VALENTINE
Will not chambermaids lie, Vincent?

VINCENT
Will not Ranger lie, Valentine?

VALENTINE
The circumstances of his story proved it true.

VINCENT
Do you think so old a master in the faculty as he will want the varnish of probability for his lies?

VALENTINE
Do you think a woman, having the advantage of her sex, and education under such a mistress, will want impudence to disavow a truth that might be prejudicial to that mistress?

VINCENT
But if both testimonies are fallible, why will you needs believe his? we are apter to believe the things we would have, than those we would not.

VALENTINE
My ill luck has taught me to credit my misfortunes and doubt my happiness.

VINCENT
But fortune we know is inconstant.

VALENTINE
And all of her sex.

VINCENT
Will you judge of fortune by your experience, and not do your mistress the same justice? Go see her, and satisfy yourself and her; for if she be innocent, consider how culpable you are, not only in your censures of her, but in not seeing her since your coming.

VALENTINE
If she be innocent, I should be afraid to surprise her, for her sake; if false, I should be afraid to surprise her for my own.

VINCENT
To be jealous and not inquisitive is as hard as to love extremely and not to be something jealous.

VALENTINE
Inquisitiveness as seldom cures jealousy, as drinking in a fever quenches the thirst.

VINCENT
If she were at the Park last night, 'tis probable she'll not miss this. Go watch her house, see who goes out, who in; while I, in the meantime, search out Ranger: who, I'll pawn my life, upon more discourse shall avow his mistake.—Here he is; go in:—how luckily is he come!

[**VALENTINE** retires to the door behind.

[Enter **RANGER**.

Ranger, you have prevented me: I was going to look you out, between the scenes at the playhouse, the coffee-house, tennis-court, or Gifford's.

RANGER
Do you want a pretence to go to a bawdy-house?—but I have other visits to make.

VINCENT
I forget. I should rather have sought you in Christina's lodgings, ha! ha! ha!

RANGER
Well, well, I'm just come to tell you that Christina—

VINCENT
Proves not, by daylight, the kind lady you followed last night out of the Park.

RANGER
I have better news for you, to my thinking.

VINCENT
What is't?

RANGER
Not that I have been in Christina's lodging this morning; but that she'll be presently here in your lodging with me.

VALENTINE [Aside]
How!

VINCENT [Retiring, and speaking softly to **VALENTINE**]
You see now, his report was a jest, a mere jest.—
[To **RANGER**]
Well, must my lodging be your vaulting-school still? thou hast appointed a wench to come hither, I find.

RANGER
A wench! you seemed to have more reverence for Christina last night.

VINCENT
Now you talk of Christina, prithee tell me what was the meaning of thy last night's romance of Christina?

RANGER
You shall know the meaning of all when Christina comes: she'll be here presently.

VINCENT
Who will? Christina?

RANGER
Yes, Christina.

VINCENT
Ha! ha! ha!

RANGER
Incredulous envy! thou art as envious as an impotent lecher at a wedding.

VINCENT
Thou art either mad, or as vain as a Frenchman newly returned home from a campaign, or obliging England.

RANGER
Thou art as envious as a rival; but if thou art mine, there's that will make you desist;—
[Gives him a letter]
—and if you are not my rival, entrusting you with such a secret will, I know, oblige you to keep it, and assist me against all other interests.

VINCENT
Do you think I take your secret as an obligation? don't I know, lovers, travellers, and poets, will give money to be heard? But what's the paper? a lampoon upon Christina, hatched last night betwixt squire Dapperwit and you, because her maid used you scurvily?

RANGER
No, 'tis only a letter from her, to show my company was not so disgustful to her last night, but that she desires it again to-day.

VALENTINE [Aside]
A letter from her!

VINCENT
A letter from Christina!
[Reads]
—Ha! ha! ha!

RANGER
Nay, 'tis pleasant.

VINCENT
You mistake, I laugh at you, not the letter.

RANGER
I am like the winning gamester, so pleased with my luck, I will not quarrel with any who calls me a fool for't.

VINCENT
Is this the style of a woman of honour?

RANGER
It may be, for ought you know; I'm sure 'tis well if your female correspondents can read.

VINCENT
I must confess I have none of the little letters, half name or title, like your Spanish Epistles Dedicatory; but that a man so frequent in honourable intrigues as you are, should not know the summons of an impudent common woman, from that of a person of honour!

RANGER
Christina is so much a person of honour she'll own what she has writ when she comes.

VINCENT
But will she come hither indeed?

RANGER
Immediately. You'll excuse my liberty with you; I could not conceal such a happiness from such a friend as you, lest you should have taken it unkindly.

VINCENT
Faith, you have obliged me indeed; for you and others would often have made me believe your honourable intrigues, but never did me the honour to convince me of 'em before.

RANGER
You are merry, I find, yet.

VINCENT
When you are happy I cannot be otherwise.

RANGER [Aside]
But I lose time; I should lay a little parson in ambush, that lives hard by, in case Christina should be impatient to be revenged of her friends, as it often happens with a discontented heiress. Women, like old soldiers, more nimbly execute than they resolve.

[Going out.

VINCENT
What now! you will not disappoint a woman of Christina's quality?

RANGER
I'll be here before she comes, I warrant you.

[Exit.

VINCENT
I do believe you truly!—What think you, Valentine?

VALENTINE [Coming forward]
I think, since she has the courage to challenge him, she'll have the honour of being first in the field.

VINCENT
Fy, your opinion of her must be as bad, as Ranger's of himself is good, to think she would write to him. I long till his bona-roba comes, that you may be both disabused.

VALENTINE
And I have not patience to stay her coming, lest you should be disabused.

[Enter **CHRISTINA** and **ISABEL**.

VINCENT
Here she is, i'faith; I'm glad she's come.

VALENTINE
And I'm sorry. But I will to my post again, lest she should say she came to me.

[Retires as before.

VINCENT [Aside]
By heavens, Christina herself! 'tis she!

[**CHRISTINA** pulls off her mask.

VALENTINE [Aside]
'Tis she:—cursed be these eyes! more cursed than when they first betrayed me to that false bewitching face.

CHRISTINA
You may wonder, sir, to see me here—

VINCENT
I must confess I do.

CHRISTINA
But the confidence your friend has in you is the cause of mine; and yet some blushes it does cost me to come to seek a man.

VALENTINE [Aside]

Modest creature!

VINCENT [Aside]
How am I deceived!

CHRISTINA
Where is he, sir? why does he not appear, to keep me in countenance? pray call him, sir; 'tis something hard if he should know I'm here.

VINCENT
I hardly can myself believe you are here, madam.

CHRISTINA
If my visit be troublesome or unseasonable, 'tis your friend's fault; I designed it not to you, sir. Pray call him out, that he may excuse it, and take it on himself, together with my shame.

VINCENT [Aside]
How impatient she is!

CHRISTINA
Or do you delay the happiness I ask, to make it more welcome? I have stayed too long for it already, and cannot more desire it. Dear sir, call him out. Where is he? above, or here within? I'll snatch the favour which you will not give.—

[Goes to the door and discovers **VALENTINE**.

What! Do you hide yourself for shame?

VALENTINE [Coming forward]
I must confess I do.

CHRISTINA
To see me come hither—

VALENTINE
I acknowledge it.

[**VALENTINE** offers to go out.

CHRISTINA
Before you came to me? But whither do you go? come, I can forgive you.

VALENTINE
But I cannot forgive you.

CHRISTINA
Whither do you go? you need not forge a quarrel to prevent mine to you: nor need you try if I would follow you, you know I will;—I have, you see.

VALENTINE [Aside]
That impudence should look so like innocence!

CHRISTINA
Whither would you go? why would you go?

VALENTINE
To call your servant to you.

CHRISTINA
She is here; what would you have with her?

VALENTINE
I mean your lover,—the man you came to meet.

CHRISTINA
Oh heavens! what lover? what man? I came to see no man but you, whom I had too long lost.

VALENTINE
You could not know that I was here.

CHRISTINA
Ask her; 'twas she that told me.

[Points to **ISABEL**.

VALENTINE
How could she know?

CHRISTINA
That you shall know hereafter.

VALENTINE
No, you thought me too far out of the way to disturb your assignation; and I assure you, madam, 'twas my ill-fortune, not my design: and that it may appear so, I do withdraw, as in all good breeding and civility I am obliged; for sure your wished-for lover's coming.

CHRISTINA
What do you mean? are you a-weary of that title?

VALENTINE
I am ashamed of it, since it grows common.

[Going out.

CHRISTINA
Nay, you will not, shall not go.

VALENTINE
My stay might give him jealousy, and so do you injury, and him the greatest in the world: heavens forbid! I would not make a man jealous; for though you call a thousand vows, and oaths, and tears to witness (as you safely may), that you have not the least of love for me, yet if he ever knew how I have loved you, sure he would not, could not believe you.

CHRISTINA
I do confess, your riddle is too hard for me to solve; therefore you are obliged to do't yourself.

VALENTINE
I wish it were capable of any other interpretation than what you know already.

CHRISTINA
Is this that generous good Valentine? who has disguised him so?

[Weeps.

VINCENT
Nay, I must withhold you then.

[Stops **VALENTINE** going out.

Methinks she should be innocent; her tongue, and eyes, together with that flood that swells 'em, do vindicate her heart.

VALENTINE
They show but their long practice of dissimulation.

[Going out.

VINCENT
Come back: I hear Ranger coming up: stay but till he comes.

VALENTINE
Do you think I have the patience of an alderman?

VINCENT
You may go out this way, when you will, by the back-stairs; but stay a little, till—Oh, here he comes.

[Re-enter **RANGER**. Upon his entrance **CHRISTINA** puts on her mask.

VALENTINE
My revenge will now detain me.

[**VALENTINE** retires again.

RANGER [Aside]

—What, come already! where is Dapperwit?—
[Aloud]
The blessing's double that comes quickly; I did not yet expect you here, otherwise I had not done myself the injury to be absent. But I hope, madam, I have not made you stay long for me.

CHRISTINA
I have not staid at all for you.

RANGER
I am glad of it, madam.

CHRISTINA [To **ISABEL**]
Is not this that troublesome stranger who last night followed the lady into my lodgings?—
[Aside]
'Tis he.

[Removing from him to the other side.

RANGER [Aside]
Why does she remove so disdainfully from me?—
[Aloud]
I find you take it ill I was not at your coming here, madam.

CHRISTINA
Indeed I do not; you are mistaken, sir.

RANGER
Confirm me by a smile then, madam; remove that cloud, which makes me apprehend foul weather.
[Goes to take off her mask]
—Mr. Vincent, pray retire; 'tis you keep on the lady's mask, and no displeasure which she has for me.—Yet, madam, you need not distrust his honour or his faith.—But do not keep the lady under constraint; pray leave us a little, Master Vincent.

CHRISTINA
You must not leave us, sir; would you leave me with a stranger?

VALENTINE [Aside]
How's that!

RANGER [Aside]
I've done amiss, I find, to bring her hither.—
[Apart to **CHRISTINA**]
—Madam, I understand you—

CHRISTINA
Sir, I do not understand you.

RANGER

You would not be known to Mr. Vincent.

CHRISTINA
'Tis your acquaintance I would avoid.

RANGER [Aside]
Dull brute that I was, to bring her hither!—
[Softly to her]
I have found my error, madam; give me but a new appointment, where I may meet you by and by, and straight I will withdraw as if I knew you not.

CHRISTINA
Why, do you know me?

RANGER [Aside]
I must not own it.—No, madam, but—[Offers to whisper].

CHRISTINA
Whispering, sir, argues an old acquaintance; but I have not the vanity to be thought of yours, and resolve you shall never have the disparagement of mine.—Mr. Vincent, pray let us go in here.

RANGER [Aside]
How's this! I am undone, I see; but if I let her go thus, I shall be an eternal laughing-stock to Vincent.

VINCENT
Do you not know him, madam? I thought you had come hither on purpose to meet him.

CHRISTINA
To meet him!

VINCENT
By your own appointment.

CHRISTINA
What strange infatuation does delude you all? you know, he said he did not know me.

VINCENT
You writ to him; he has your letter.

CHRISTINA
Then, you know my name sure? yet you confessed but now you knew me not.

RANGER
I must confess your anger has disguised you more than your mask: for I thought to have met a kinder Christina here.

CHRISTINA [Aside]

Heavens! how could he know me in this place? he watched me hither sure; or is there any other of my name.—
[Aloud]
That you may no longer mistake me for your Christina, I'll pull off that which soothes your error.

[Pulls off her mask.

RANGER
Take but t'other vizard off too, (I mean your anger,) and I'll swear you are the same, and only Christina which I wished, and thought, to meet here.

CHRISTINA
How could you think to meet me here?

RANGER [Gives her the letter]
By virtue of this your commission; which now, I see, was meant a real challenge: for you look as if you would fight with me.

CHRISTINA
The paper is a stranger to me; I never writ it. You are abused.

VINCENT
Christina is a person of honour, and will own what she has written, Ranger.

RANGER [Aside]
So! the comedy begins; I shall be laughed at sufficiently if I do not justify myself; I must set my impudence to hers. She is resolved to deny all, I see, and I have lost all hope of her.

VINCENT
Come, faith, Ranger—

RANGER
You will deny too, madam, that I followed you last night from the Park to your lodging, where I staid with you till morning? you never saw me before, I warrant.

CHRISTINA
That you rudely intruded last night into my lodging, I cannot deny; but I wonder you have the confidence to brag of it: sure you will not of your reception?

RANGER
I never was so ill-bred as to brag of my reception in a lady's chamber; not a word of that, madam.

VALENTINE [Aside]
How! If he lies, I revenge her; if it I be true, I revenge myself.

[**VALENTINE** draws his sword, which **VINCENT**, seeing, thrusts him back, and shuts the door upon him before he is discovered by **RANGER**.

[Enter **LYDIA** and **LEONORE**, stopping at the door.

LYDIA
What do I see! Christina with him! a counterplot to mine, to make me and it ridiculous. 'Tis true, I find, they have been long acquainted, and I long abused; but since she intends a triumph, in spite, as well as shame, (not emulation,) I retire. She deserves no envy, who will be shortly in my condition; his natural inconstancy will prove my best revenge on her—on both.

[Exeunt **LYDIA** and **LEONORE**.

[Enter **DAPPERWIT**.

DAPPERWIT
Christina's going away again;—what's the matter?

RANGER
What do you mean?

DAPPERWIT
I scarce had paid the chairmen, and was coming up after her, but I met her on the stairs, in as much haste as if she had been frightened.

RANGER
Who do you talk of?

DAPPERWIT
Christina, whom I took up in a chair just now at St. James's gate.

RANGER
Thou art mad! here she is, this is Christina.

DAPPERWIT
I must confess I did not see her face; but I am sure the lady is gone that I brought just now.

RANGER
I tell you again this is she: did you bring two?

CHRISTINA
I came in no chair, had no guide but my woman there.

VINCENT
When did you bring your lady, Dapperwit?

DAPPERWIT
Even now, just now.

VINCENT
This lady has been here half-an-hour.

RANGER
He knows not what he says, he is mad: you are all so; I am so too.

VINCENT
'Tis the best excuse you can make for yourself, and by owning your mistake you'll show you are come to yourself. I myself saw your woman at the door, who but looked in, and then immediately went down again;—as your friend Dapperwit too affirms.

CHRISTINA
You had best follow her that looked for you; and I'll go seek out him I came to see.—Mr. Vincent, pray let me in here.

RANGER
'Tis very fine! wondrous fine!

[**CHRISTINA** goes out a little, and returns.

CHRISTINA
Oh! he is gone! Mr. Vincent, follow him; he were yet more severe to me in endangering his life, than in his censures against me. You know the power of his enemies is great as their malice;—just Heaven preserve him from them, and me from this ill or unlucky man!

[Exeunt **CHRISTINA**, **ISABEL**, and **VINCENT**.

RANGER
'Tis well—nay, certainly, I shall never be master of my senses more: but why dost thou help to distract me too?

DAPPERWIT
My astonishment was as great as yours to see her go away again; I would have stayed her if I could.

RANGER
Yet again talking of a woman you met going out, when I talk of Christina!

DAPPERWIT
I talk of Christina too.

RANGER
She went out just now; the woman you found me with was she.

DAPPERWIT
That was not the Christina I brought just now.

RANGER
You brought her almost half an hour ago;—'sdeath, will you give me the lie?

DAPPERWIT

A lady disappointed by her gallant, the night before her journey, could not be more touchy with her maid or husband, than you are with me now after your disappointment; but if you thank me so, I'll go serve myself hereafter. For aught I know, I have disappointed Mrs. Martha for you, and may lose thirty thousand pounds by the bargain. Farewell! a raving lover is fit for solitude.

[Exit.

RANGER

Lydia, triumph! I now am thine again. Of intrigues, honourable or dishonourable, and all sorts of rambling, I take my leave; when we are giddy, 'tis time to stand still. Why should we be so fond of the by-paths of love, where we are still waylaid with surprises, trepans, dangers, and murdering disappointments?—

Just as at blindman's buff we run at all,   Whilst those that lead us laugh to see us fall;   And when we think we hold the lady fast,   We find it but her scarf, or veil, at last.

[Exit.

ACT THE FIFTH

SCENE I.—St. James's Park

Enter **DAPPERWIT** and **SIR SIMON ADDLEPLOT**, the latter leading **MRS MARTHA**.

SIR SIMON ADDLEPLOT

At length you see I have freed the captive lady for her longing knight, Mr. Dapperwit:—who brings off a plot cleverly now?

DAPPERWIT

I wish our poets were half so good at it.—Mrs. Martha, a thousand welcomes!

[**DAPPERWIT** kisses and embraces **MRS MARTHA**.

SIR SIMON ADDLEPLOT

Hold, hold, sir: your joy is a little too familiar, faith and troth!

DAPPERWIT

Will you not let me salute Mrs. Martha?

MRS MARTHA

What, Jonas, do you think I do not know good breeding? must I be taught by you?

SIR SIMON ADDLEPLOT

I would have kept the maidenhead of your lips for your sweet knight, Mrs. Martha, that's all; I dare swear you never kissed any man before but your father.

MRS MARTHA
My sweet knight, if he will be knight of mine, must be contented with what he finds, as well as other knights.

SIR SIMON ADDLEPLOT
So smart already, faith and troth!

MRS MARTHA
Dear Mr. Dapperwit I am overjoyed to see you; but I thank honest Jonas for't.

[She hugs **DAPPERWIT**.

SIR SIMON ADDLEPLOT [Aside]
How she hugs him!

MRS MARTHA
Poor Mr. Dapperwit, I thought I should never have seen you again; but I thank honest Jonas there—

SIR SIMON ADDLEPLOT
Do not thank me, Mrs. Martha, any more than I thank you.

MRS MARTHA
I would not be ungrateful, Jonas.

SIR SIMON ADDLEPLOT
Then reserve your kindness only for your worthy, noble, brave, heroic knight, who loves you only, and only deserves your kindness.

MRS MARTHA
I will show my kindness to my worthy, brave, heroic knight, in being kind to his friend, his dear friend, who helped him to me.

[Hugs **DAPPERWIT** again.

SIR SIMON ADDLEPLOT
But, Mistress Martha, he is not to help him always; though he helps him to be married, he is not to help him when he is married.

MRS MARTHA
What, Mr. Dapperwit, will you love my worthy knight less after marriage than before? that were against the custom; for marriage gets a man friends, instead of losing those he has.

DAPPERWIT
I will ever be his servant and yours, dear madam; do not doubt me.

MRS MARTHA
I do not, sweet dear Mr. Dapperwit; but I should not have seen you these two days if it had not been for honest Jonas there—

[She kisses **DAPPERWIT**.

SIR SIMON ADDLEPLOT [Apart to **DAPPERWIT**]
For shame! though she be young and foolish, do not you wrong me to my face.

DAPPERWIT
Would you have me so ill bred as to repulse her innocent kindness?—what a thing it is to want wit!

SIR SIMON ADDLEPLOT [Aside]
A pox! I must make haste to discover myself, or I shall discover what I would not discover; but if I should discover myself in this habit, 'twould not be to my advantage. But I'll go, put on my own clothes, and look like a knight.—
[Aloud]
Well, Mrs. Martha, I'll go seek out your knight: are you not impatient to see him?

MRS MARTHA
Wives must be obedient; let him take his own time.

SIR SIMON ADDLEPLOT
Can you trust yourself a turn or two with Master Dapperwit?

MRS MARTHA
Yes, yes, Jonas—as long as you will.

SIR SIMON ADDLEPLOT [Aside]
But I would not trust you with him, if I could help it.—

So married wight sees what he dares not blame;   And cannot budge for fear, nor stay for shame.

[Exit.

DAPPERWIT
I am glad he is gone, that I may laugh. 'Tis such a miracle of fops, that his conversation should be pleasant to me, even when it hindered me of yours.

MRS MARTHA
Indeed, I'm glad he is gone too, as pleasant as he is.

DAPPERWIT
I know why, I know why, sweet Mrs. Martha. I warrant you, you had rather have the parson's company than his?—now you are out of your father's house, 'tis time to leave being a hypocrite.

MRS MARTHA
Well, for the jest's sake, to disappoint my knight, I would not care if I disappointed myself of a ladyship.

DAPPERWIT

Come, I will not keep you on the tenters; I know you have a mind to make sure of me: I have a little chaplain (I wish he were a bishop or one of the friars) to perfect our revenge upon that zealous Jew, your father.

MRS MARTHA
Do not speak ill of my father; he has been your friend, I'm sure.

DAPPERWIT
My friend!

MRS MARTHA
His hard usage of me conspired with your good mien and wit, and to avoid slavery unto him, I stoop to your yoke.

DAPPERWIT
I will be obliged to your father for nothing but a portion; nor to you for your love; 'twas due to my merit.

MRS MARTHA
You show yourself Sir Simon's original; if 'twere not for that vanity—

DAPPERWIT
I should be no wit—'tis the badge of my calling; for you can no more find a man of wit without vanity than a fine woman without affectation: but let us go before the knight comes again.

MRS MARTHA
Let us go before my father comes; he soon will have the intelligence.

DAPPERWIT
Stay, let me think a little.

[Pauses.

MRS MARTHA
What are you thinking of? you should have thought before this time, or I should have thought rather.

DAPPERWIT
Peace! peace!

MRS MARTHA
What are you thinking of?

DAPPERWIT
I am thinking what a wit without vanity is like. He is like—

MRS MARTHA
You do not think we are in a public place, and may be surprised and prevented by my father's scouts!

DAPPERWIT

What! would you have me lose my thought?

MRS MARTHA
You would rather lose your mistress, it seems.

DAPPERWIT
He is like—I think I am a sot to-night, let me perish.

MRS MARTHA
Nay, if you are so in love with your thought—

[Offers to go.

DAPPERWIT
Are you so impatient to be my wife?—He is like—he is like—a picture without shadows, or—or—a face without patches—or a diamond without a foil. These are new thoughts now, these are new!

MRS MARTHA
You are wedded already to your thoughts, I see;—good night.

DAPPERWIT
Madam, do not take it ill:—
For loss of happy thought there's no amends;
For his new jest true wit will lose old friends.
That's new again,—the thought's new.

[Exeunt.

SCENE II.—Another part of the same

Enter **GRIPE**, leading **LUCY**; **MRS JOYNER** and **MRS CROSSBITE** following.

GRIPE
Mrs. Joyner, I can conform to this mode of public walking by moonlight, because one is not known.

LUCY
Why, are you ashamed of your company?

GRIPE
No, pretty one; because in the dark, or as it were in the dark, there is no envy nor scandal. I would neither lose you nor my reputation.

MRS JOYNER
Your reputation! indeed, your worship, 'tis well known there are as grave men as your worship; nay, men in office too, that adjourn their cares and businesses, to come and unbend themselves at night here, with a little vizard-mask.

GRIPE
I do believe it, Mrs. Joyner.

LUCY
Ay, godmother, and carries and treats her at Mulberry-garden.

MRS CROSSBITE
Nay, does not only treat her, but gives her his whole gleaning of that day.

GRIPE
They may, they may, Mrs. Crossbite; they take above six in the hundred.

MRS CROSSBITE
Nay, there are those of so much worth and honour and love, that they'll take it from their wives and children to give it to their misses; now your worship has no wife, and but one child.

GRIPE [Aside]
Still for my edification!

MRS JOYNER
That's true, indeed; for I know a great lady that cannot follow her husband abroad to his haunts, because her Ferrandine is so ragged and greasy, whilst his mistress is as fine as fi'pence, in embroidered satins.

GRIPE
Politicly done of him indeed! If the truth were known, he is a statesman by that, umph—

MRS CROSSBITE
Truly, your women of quality are very troublesome to their husbands: I have heard 'em complain, they will allow them no separate maintenance, though the honourable jilts themselves will not marry without it.

MRS JOYNER
Come, come, mistress; sometimes 'tis the craft of those gentlemen to complain of their wives' expenses to excuse their own narrowness to their misses; but your daughter has a gallant that can make no excuse.

GRIPE
So, Mrs. Joyner!—my friend, Mrs. Joyner—

MRS CROSSBITE
I hope, indeed, he'll give my daughter no cause to dun him; for, poor wretch! she is as modest as her mother.

GRIPE
I profess, I believe it.

LUCY
But I have the boldness to ask him for a treat.—Come, gallant, we must walk towards the Mulberry-garden.

GRIPE
So!—I am afraid, little mistress, the rooms are all taken up by this time.

MRS JOYNER [Aside to **GRIPE**]
Will you shame yourself again?

LUCY
If the rooms be full we'll have an arbour.

GRIPE
At this time of night!—besides, the waiters will ne'er come near you.

LUCY
They will be observant of good customers, as we shall be. Come along.

GRIPE
Indeed, and verily, little mistress, I would go, but that I should be forsworn if I did.

MRS JOYNER
That's so pitiful an excuse!—

GRIPE
In truth, I have forsworn the place ever since I was pawned there for a reckoning.

LUCY
You have broken many an oath for the good old cause, and will you boggle at one for your poor little miss? Come along.

[Enter **LADY FLIPPANT** behind.

LADY FLIPPANT
Unfortunate lady that I am! I have left the herd on purpose to be chased, and have wandered this hour here; but the Park affords not so much as a satyr for me, and (that's strange!) no Burgundy man or drunken scourer will reel my way. The rag-women, and cinder-women, have better luck than I.—But who are these? if this mongrel light does not deceive me, 'tis my brother,—'tis he:—there's Joyner, too, and two other women. I'll follow 'em. It must be he, for this world hath nothing like him;—I know not what the devil may be in the other.

[Exeunt.

SCENE III.—Another part of the same

Enter **SIR SIMON ADDLEPLOT**, *in fine clothes*, **DAPPERWIT** *and* **MRS MARTHA**, *unseen by him at the door.*

SIR SIMON ADDLEPLOT
Well, after all my seeking, I can find those I would not find; I'm sure 'twas old Gripe, and Joyner with him, and the widow followed. He would not have been here, but to have sought his daughter, sure; but vigilant Dapperwit has spied them too, and has, no doubt, secured her from him.

DAPPERWIT [Aside]
And you.

SIR SIMON ADDLEPLOT
The rogue is as good at hiding, as I am at stealing, a mistress. 'Tis a vain, conceited fellow, yet I think 'tis an honest fellow:—but, again, he is a damnable whoring fellow; and what opportunity this air and darkness may incline 'em to, Heaven knows; for I have heard the rogue say himself, a lady will no more show her modesty in the dark than a Spaniard his courage.

DAPPERWIT
Ha! ha! ha!—

SIR SIMON ADDLEPLOT
Nay, if you are there, my true friend, I'll forgive your hearkening, if you'll forgive my censures.—I speak to you, dear Madam Martha; dear, dear—behold your worthy knight—

MRS MARTHA
That's far from neighbours.

SIR SIMON ADDLEPLOT
Is come to reap the fruit of his labours.

MRS MARTHA
I cannot see the knight; well, but I'm sure I hear Jonas.

SIR SIMON ADDLEPLOT
I am no Jonas, Mrs. Martha.

MRS MARTHA
The night is not so dark, nor the peruke so big, but I can discern Jonas.

SIR SIMON ADDLEPLOT
Faith and troth, I am the very Sir Simon Addleplot that is to marry you; the same Dapperwit solicited you for; ask him else, my name is not Jonas.

MRS MARTHA
You think my youth and simplicity capable of this cheat; but let me tell you, Jonas, 'tis not your borrowed clothes and titles shall make me marry my father's man.

SIR SIMON ADDLEPLOT

Borrowed title! I'll be sworn I bought it of my laundress, who was a court-laundress; but, indeed, my clothes I have not paid for; therefore, in that sense, they are borrowed.

MRS MARTHA
Prithee, Jonas, let the jest end, or I shall be presently in earnest.

SIR SIMON ADDLEPLOT
Pray, be in earnest, and let us go; the parson and supper stay for us, and I am a knight in earnest.

MRS MARTHA
You a knight! insolent, saucy fool.

SIR SIMON ADDLEPLOT
The devil take me, Mrs. Martha, if I am not a knight now! a knight-baronet too! A man ought, I see, to carry his patent in his pocket when he goes to be married; 'tis more necessary than a licence. I am a knight indeed and indeed now, Mrs. Martha.

MRS MARTHA
Indeed and indeed, the trick will not pass, Jonas.

SIR SIMON ADDLEPLOT
Poor wretch! she's afraid she shall not be a lady.—Come, come, discover the intrigue, Dapperwit.

MRS MARTHA
You need not discover the intrigue, 'tis apparent already. Unworthy Mr. Dapperwit, after my confidence reposed in you, could you be so little generous as to betray me to my father's man? but I'll be even with you.

SIR SIMON ADDLEPLOT
Do not accuse him, poor man! before you hear him.—Tell her the intrigue, man.

DAPPERWIT
A pox! she will not believe us.

SIR SIMON ADDLEPLOT
Will you not excuse yourself? but I must not let it rest so.—Know, then, Mrs. Martha—

MRS MARTHA
Come, I forgive thee before thy confession, Jonas; you never had had the confidence to have designed this cheat upon me but from Mr. Dapperwit's encouragement—'twas his plot.

SIR SIMON ADDLEPLOT
Nay, do not do me that wrong, madam.

MRS MARTHA
But since he has trepanned me out of my father's house, he is like to keep me as long as I live; and so good night, Jonas.

SIR SIMON ADDLEPLOT
Hold, hold, what d'ye mean both? prithee tell her I am Sir Simon, and no Jonas.

DAPPERWIT
A pox! she will not believe us, I tell you.

SIR SIMON ADDLEPLOT
I have provided a supper and parson at Mulberry-garden, and invited all my friends I could meet in the Park.

DAPPERWIT
Nay, rather than they shall be disappointed, there shall be a bride and bridegroom to entertain 'em; Mrs. Martha and I will go thither presently.

SIR SIMON ADDLEPLOT
Why, shall she be your bride?

DAPPERWIT
You see she will have it so.

SIR SIMON ADDLEPLOT
Will you make Dapperwit your husband?

MRS MARTHA
Rather than my father's man.

SIR SIMON ADDLEPLOT
Oh, the devil!

MRS MARTHA
Nay, come along, Jonas, you shall make one at the wedding, since you helped to contrive it.

SIR SIMON ADDLEPLOT
Will you cheat yourself, for fear of being cheated?

MRS MARTHA
I am desperate now.

SIR SIMON ADDLEPLOT
Wilt thou let her do so ill a thing, Dapperwit, as to marry thee? open her eyes, prithee, and tell her I am a true knight.

DAPPERWIT
'Twould be in vain, by my life! you have carried yourself so like a natural clerk—and so adieu, good Jonas.

[Exeunt **MRS MARTHA** and **DAPPERWIT**.

SIR SIMON ADDLEPLOT

What! ruined by my own plot, like an old cavalier! yet like him, too, I will plot on still, a plot of prevention. So! I have it—her father was here even now, I'm sure; well—I'll go tell her father of her, that I will!
And punish so her folly and his treachery:
Revenge is sweet, and makes amends for lechery.

[Exit.

SCENE IV.—Another part of the same

Enter **LYDIA** and **LEONORE**.

LYDIA
I wish I had not come hither to-night, Leonore.

LEONORE
Why did you, madam, if the place be so disagreeable to you?

LYDIA
We cannot help visiting the place often where we have lost anything we value: I lost Ranger here last night.

LEONORE
You thought you had lost him before, a great while ago; and therefore you ought to be the less troubled.

LYDIA
But 'twas here I missed him first, I'm sure.

LEONORE
Come, madam, let not the loss vex you; he is not worth the looking after.

LYDIA
It cannot but vex me yet, if I lost him by my own fault.

LEONORE
You had but too much care to keep him.

LYDIA
It often happens, indeed, that too much care is as bad as negligence; but I had rather be robbed than lose what I have carelessly.

LEONORE
But, I believe you would hang the thief if you could.

LYDIA

Not if I could have my own again.

LEONORE
I see you would be too merciful.

LYDIA
I wish I were tried.

LEONORE
But, madam, if you please, we will waive the discourse; for people seldom (I suppose) talk with pleasure of their real losses.

LYDIA
'Tis better than to ruminate on them; mine, I'm sure, will not out of head nor heart.

LEONORE
Grief is so far from retrieving a loss, that it makes it greater; but the way to lessen it is by a comparison with others' losses. Here are ladies in the Park of your acquaintance, I doubt not, can compare with you; pray, madam, let us walk and find 'em out.

LYDIA
'Tis the resentment, you say, makes the loss great or little; and then, I'm sure, there is none like mine: however, go on.

[Exeunt.

SCENE V.—Another part of the same

Enter **VINCENT** and **VALENTINE**.

VINCENT
I am glad I have found you, for now I am prepared to lead you out of the dark and all your trouble: I have good news.

VALENTINE
You are as unmerciful as the physician who with new arts keeps his miserable patient alive and in hopes, when he knows the disease is incurable.

VINCENT
And you, like the melancholy patient, mistrust and hate your physician, because he will not comply with your despair: but I'll cure your jealousy now.

VALENTINE
You know, all diseases grow worse by relapses.

VINCENT

Trust me once more.

VALENTINE
Well, you may try your experiments upon me.

VINCENT
Just as I shut the door upon you, the woman Ranger expected came up stairs; but finding another woman in discourse with him, went down again; I suppose, as jealous of him, as you of Christina.

VALENTINE
How does it appear she came to Ranger?

VINCENT
Thus: Dapperwit came up after he had brought her, just then, in a chair from St. James's by Ranger's appointment; and it is certain your Christina came to you.

VALENTINE
How can that be? for she knew not I was in the kingdom.

VINCENT
My man confesses, when I sent him to inquire of her woman about her lady's being here in the Park last night, he told her you were come; and she, it seems, told her mistress.

VALENTINE [Aside]
That might be.—
[Aloud]
But did not Christina confess, Ranger was in her lodging last night?

VINCENT
By intrusion, which she had more particularly informed me of, if her apprehensions of your danger had not posted me after you; she not having yet (as I suppose) heard of Clerimont's recovery. I left her, poor creature! at home, distracted with a thousand fears for your life and love.

VALENTINE
Her love, I'm sure, has cost me more fears than my life; yet that little danger is not past (as you think) till the great one be over.

VINCENT
Open but your eyes, and the fantastic goblin's vanished, and all your idle fears will turn to shame; for jealousy is the basest cowardice.

VALENTINE
I had rather, indeed, blush for myself than her.

VINCENT
I'm sure you will have more reason. But is not that Ranger there?

[Enter **RANGER**, followed by **CHRISTINA** and **ISABEL**; after them **LYDIA** and **LEONORE**.

VALENTINE
I think it is.

VINCENT
I suppose his friend Dapperwit is not far off; I will examine them both before you, and not leave you so much as the shadow of doubt: Ranger's astonishment at my lodging confessed his mistake.

VALENTINE
His astonishment might proceed from Christina's unexpected strangeness to him.

VINCENT
He shall satisfy you now himself to the contrary, I warrant you; have but patience.

VALENTINE
I had rather, indeed, he should satisfy my doubts than my revenge; therefore I can have patience.

VINCENT
But what women are those that follow him?

VALENTINE
Stay a little—

RANGER
Lydia, Lydia—poor Lydia!

LYDIA [To **LEONORE**]
If she be my rival, 'tis some comfort yet to see her follow him, rather than he her.

LEONORE
But if you follow them a little longer, for your comfort you shall see them go hand in hand.

CHRISTINA [To **RANGER**]
Sir! sir!—.

LEONORE
She calls to him already.

LYDIA
But he does not hear, you see; let us go a little nearer.

VINCENT
Sure it is Ranger!

VALENTINE
As sure as the woman that follows him closest is Christina.

VINCENT

For shame! talk not of Christina; I left her just now at home, surrounded with so many fears and griefs she could not stir.

VALENTINE
She is come, it may be, to divert them here in the Park; I'm sure 'tis she.

VINCENT
When the moon, at this instant, scarce affords light enough to distinguish a man from a tree, how can you know her?

VALENTINE
How can you know Ranger, then?

VINCENT
I heard him speak.

VALENTINE
So you may her too, I'll secure you, if you will draw but a little nearer; she came, doubtless, to no other end but to speak with him: observe—

CHRISTINA [To **RANGER**]
Sir, I have followed you hitherto; but now, I must desire you to follow me out of the company; for I would not be overheard nor disturbed.

RANGER
Ha! is not this Christina's voice? it is, I am sure; I cannot be deceived now.—Dear madam—

VINCENT
It is she indeed. [Apart to **VALENTINE**.

VALENTINE
Is it so?

CHRISTINA [To **RANGER**]
Come, sir—.

VALENTINE [Aside]
Nay, I'll follow you too, though not invited.

LYDIA [Aside]
I must not, cannot stay behind.

[They all go off together hastily.

[Re-enter **CHRISTINA**, **ISABEL**, and **VALENTINE** on the other side.

CHRISTINA
Come along, sir.

VALENTINE [Aside]
So! I must stick to her when all is done; her new servant has lost her in the crowd, she has gone too fast for him; so much my revenge is swifter than his love. Now shall I not only have the deserted lover's revenge, of disappointing her of her new man, but an opportunity infallibly at once to discover her falseness, and confront her impudence.

CHRISTINA
Pray come along, sir, I am in haste.

VALENTINE [Aside]
So eager, indeed!—I wish that cloud may yet withhold the moon, that this false woman may not discover me before I do her.

CHRISTINA
Here no one can hear us, and I'm sure we cannot see one another.

VALENTINE [Aside]
'Sdeath! what have I giddily run myself upon? 'Tis rather a trial of myself than her;—I cannot undergo it.

CHRISTINA
Come nearer, sir.

VALENTINE [Aside]
Hell and vengeance! I cannot suffer it—I cannot.

CHRISTINA
Come, come; yet nearer,—pray come nearer.

VALENTINE [Aside]
It is impossible! I cannot hold! I must discover myself, rather than her infamy.

CHRISTINA [Speaks, walking slowly]
You are conscious, it seems, of the wrong you have done me, and are ashamed, though in the dark.

VALENTINE [Aside]
How's this!

CHRISTINA
I'm glad to find it so; for all my business with you is, to show you your late mistakes, and force a confession from you of those unmannerly injuries you have done me.

VALENTINE [Aside]
What! I think she's honest; or does she know me?—sure she cannot.

CHRISTINA
First, your intrusion, last night, into my lodging; which, I suppose, has begot your other gross mistakes.

VALENTINE [Aside]
No, she takes me for Ranger, I see again.

CHRISTINA
You are to know, then, (since needs you must,) it was not me you followed last night to my lodging from the Park, but some kinswoman of yours, it seems, whose fear of being discovered by you prevailed with me to personate her, while she withdrew, our habits and our statures being much alike; which I did with as much difficulty, as she used importunity to make me; and all this my Lady Flippant can witness, who was then with your cousin.

VALENTINE [Aside]
I am glad to hear this.

CHRISTINA
Now, what your claim to me, at Mr. Vincent's lodging, meant; the letter and promises you unworthily, or erroneously, laid to my charge, you must explain to me and others, or—

VALENTINE [Aside]
How's this! I hope I shall discover no guilt but my own:—she would not speak in threats to a lover.

CHRISTINA
Was it because you found me in Mr. Vincent's lodgings you took a liberty to use me like one of your common visitants? but know, I came no more to Mr. Vincent than you. Yet, I confess, my visit was intended to a man—a brave man, till you made him use a woman ill; worthy the love of a princess, till you made him censure mine; good as angels, till you made him unjust:—why, in the name of honour, would you do't?

VALENTINE [Aside]
How happily am I disappointed!—poor injured Christina!

CHRISTINA
He would have sought me out first, if you had not made him fly from me. Our mutual love, confirmed by a contract, made our hearts inseparable, till you rudely, if not maliciously, thrust in upon us, and broke the close and happy knot: I had lost him before for a month, now for ever.

[Weeps.

VALENTINE [Aside]
My joy and pity makes me as mute as my shame; yet I must discover myself.

CHRISTINA
Your silence is a confession of your guilt.

VALENTINE [Aside]
I own it.

CHRISTINA

But that will not serve my turn; for straight you must go clear yourself and me to him you have injured in me! if he has not made too much haste from me to be found again. You must, I say; for he is a man that will have satisfaction; and in satisfying him, you do me.

VALENTINE
Then he is satisfied.

CHRISTINA
How! is it you? then I am not satisfied.

VALENTINE
Will you be worse than your word?

CHRISTINA
I gave it not to you.

VALENTINE
Come, dear Christina, the jealous, like the drunkard, has his punishment with his offence.

[Re-enter **VINCENT**.

VINCENT
Valentine! Mr. Valentine!

VALENTINE
Vincent!—

VINCENT
Where have you been all this while?

[**VALENTINE** holds **CHRISTINA** by the hand; who seems to struggle to get from him.

VALENTINE
Here with my injured Christina.

VINCENT
She's behind with Ranger, who is forced to speak all the tender things himself; for she affords him not a word.

VALENTINE
Pish! pish! Vincent; who is blind now? who deceived now?

VINCENT
You are; for I'm sure Christina is with him. Come back and see.

[They go out on one side, and return on the other.

[Re-enter **LYDIA** and **LEONORE**, followed by **RANGER**.

RANGER [To **LYDIA**]
Still mocked! still abused! did you not bid me follow you where we might not be disturbed or overheard?—and now not allow me a word!

VINCENT [Apart to **VALENTINE**]
Did you hear him?

VALENTINE [Apart to **VINCENT**]
Yes, yes, peace.

RANGER
Disowning your letter and me at Mr. Vincent's lodging, declaring you came to meet another there, and not me, with a great deal of such affronting unkindness, might be reasonable enough, because you would not entrust Vincent with our love; but now, when nobody sees us nor hears us, why this unseasonable shyness?

LYDIA [Aside]
It seems she did not expect him there, but had appointed to meet another:—I wish it were so.

RANGER
I have not patience!—do you design thus to revenge my intrusion into your lodging last night? sure if you had then been displeased with my company, you would not have invited yourself to't again by a letter? or is this a punishment for bringing you to a house so near your own, where, it seems, you were known too? I do confess it was a fault; but make me suffer any penance but your silence, because it is the certain mark of a mistress's lasting displeasure.

LYDIA [Aside]
My—is not yet come.

RANGER
Not yet a word! you did not use me so unkindly last night, when you chid me out of your house, and with indignation bid me begone. Now, you bid me follow you, and yet will have nothing to say to me; and I am more deceived this day and night than I was last night;—when, I must confess, I followed you for another—

LYDIA [Aside]
I'm glad to hear that.

RANGER
One that would have used me better; whose love I have ungratefully abused for yours; yet from no other reason but my natural inconstancy.—
[Aside]
Poor Lydia! Lydia!

LYDIA [Aside]
He muttered my name sure; and with a sigh.

RANGER
But as last night by following (as I thought) her, I found you, so this night, by following you in vain, I do resolve, if I can find her again, to keep her for ever.

LYDIA [Aside]
Now I am obliged, and brought into debt, by his inconstancy:—faith, now cannot I hold out any longer; I must discover myself.

RANGER
But, madam, because I intend to see you no more, I'll take my leave of you for good and all; since you will not speak, I'll try if you will squeak.

[Goes to throw her down, she squeaks.

LYDIA
Mr. Ranger! Mr. Ranger!

VINCENT
Fy! Fy! you need not ravish Christina sure, that loves you so.

RANGER [Aside]
Is it she! Lydia all this while!—how am I gulled! and Vincent in the plot too!

LYDIA
Now, false Ranger!

RANGER
Now, false Christina too!—you thought I did not know you now, because I offered you such an unusual civility.

LYDIA
You knew me!—I warrant you knew, too, that I was the Christina you followed out of the Park last night! that I was the Christina that writ the letter too!

RANGER
Certainly, therefore I would have taken my revenge, you see, for your tricks.

VALENTINE [To **CHRISTINA**]
Is not this the same woman that took refuge in your house last night, madam?

CHRISTINA
The very same.

VALENTINE
What, Mr. Ranger, we have chopped, and changed, and hid our Christinas so long and often, that at last we have drawn each of us our own?

RANGER

Mr. Valentine in England!—the truth on't is, you have juggled together, and drawn without my knowledge; but since she will have it so, she shall wear me for good and all now.

[Goes to take her by the hand.

LYDIA
Come not near me.

RANGER
Nay, you need not be afraid I would ravish you, now I know you.

LYDIA [Apart to **LEONORE**, **RANGER** listens]
And yet, Leonore, I think 'tis but justice to pardon the fault I made him commit?

RANGER
You consider it right, cousin; for indeed you are but merciful to yourself in it.

LYDIA
Yet, if I would be rigorous, though I made a blot, your oversight has lost the game.

RANGER
But 'twas rash woman's play, cousin, and ought not to be played again, let me tell you.

[Enter **DAPPERWIT**.

DAPPERWIT
Who's there? who's there?

RANGER
Dapperwit.

DAPPERWIT
Mr. Ranger, I am glad I have met with you, for I have left my bride just now in the house at Mulberry-garden, to come and pick up some of my friends in the Park here to sup with us.

RANGER
Your bride! are you married then? where is your bride?

DAPPERWIT
Here at Mulberry-garden, I say, where you, these ladies and gentlemen, shall all be welcome, if you will afford me the honour of your company.

RANGER
With all our hearts:—but who have you married? Lucy?

DAPPERWIT
What! do you think I would marry a wench? I have married an heiress worth thirty thousand pounds, let me perish!

VINCENT
An heiress worth thirty thousand pounds!

DAPPERWIT
Mr. Vincent, your servant; you here too?

RANGER
Nay, we are more of your acquaintance here, I think.—Go, we'll follow you, for if you have not dismissed your parson, perhaps we may make him more work.

[Exeunt.

SCENE VI.—The Dining-room in Mulberry-garden House

Enter **SIR SIMON ADDLEPLOT**, **GRIPE**, **LADY FLIPPANT**, **MRS MARTHA**, **MRS JOYNER**, **MRS CROSSBITE**, and **LUCY**.

SIR SIMON ADDLEPLOT
'Tis as I told you, sir, you see.

GRIPE
Oh, graceless babe! married to a wit! an idle, loitering, slandering, foul-mouthed, beggarly wit! Oh that my child should ever live to marry a wit!

MRS JOYNER
Indeed, your worship had better seen her fairly buried, as they say.

MRS CROSSBITE
If my daughter there should have done so, I would not have given her a groat.

GRIPE
Marry a wit!

SIR SIMON ADDLEPLOT [Aside to **MRS JOYNER**]
Mrs. Joyner, do not let me lose the widow too:—for if you do, (betwixt friends,) I and my small annuity are both blown up: it will follow my estate.

MRS JOYNER [Aside]
I warrant you.

LADY FLIPPANT [Aside to **MRS JOYNER**]
Let us make sure of Sir Simon to-night, or—.

MRS JOYNER
You need not fear it.—

[Aside]
Like the lawyers, while my clients endeavour to cheat one another, I in justice cheat 'em both.

GRIPE
Marry a wit!

[Enter **DAPPERWIT**, **RANGER**, **LYDIA**, **VALENTINE**, **CHRISTINA**, and **VINCENT**. **DAPPERWIT** stops them, and they stand all behind.

DAPPERWIT [Aside]
What, is he here! Lucy and her mother!

GRIPE
Tell me how thou camest to marry a wit.

MRS MARTHA
Pray be not angry, sir, and I'll give you a good reason.

GRIPE
Reason for marrying a wit!

MRS MARTHA
Indeed, I found myself six months gone with child, and saw no hopes of your getting me a husband, or else I had not married a wit, sir.

MRS JOYNER
Then you were the wit.

GRIPE
Had you that reason? nay, then—

[Holding up his hands.

DAPPERWIT [Aside]
How's that!

RANGER
Who would have thought, Dapperwit, you would have married a wench?

DAPPERWIT [To **RANGER**]
—Well, thirty thousand pounds will make me amends; I have known my betters wink, and fall on for five or six.—
[To **GRIPE** and the rest]
What! you are come, sir, to give me joy? you Mrs. Lucy, you and you? well, unbid guests are doubly welcome.—Sir Simon, I made bold to invite these ladies and gentlemen.—For you must know, Mr. Ranger, this worthy Sir Simon does not only give me my wedding supper, but my mistress too; and is, as it were, my father.

SIR SIMON ADDLEPLOT
Then I am, as it were, a grandfather to your new wife's Hans en kelder; to which you are but, as it were, a father! there's for you again, sir—ha, ha!—

RANGER [To **VINCENT**]
Ha! ha! ha!—.

DAPPERWIT
Fools sometimes say unhappy things, if we would mind 'em; but—what! melancholy at your daughter's wedding, sir?

GRIPE
How deplorable is my condition!

DAPPERWIT
Nay, if you will rob me of my wench, sir, can you blame me for robbing you of your daughter? I cannot be without a woman.

GRIPE [Aside]
My daughter, my reputation, and my money gone!—but the last is dearest to me. Yet at once I may retrieve that, and be revenged for the loss of the other: and all this by marrying Lucy here: I shall get my five hundred pounds again, and get heirs to exclude my daughter and frustrate Dapperwit; besides, 'tis agreed on all hands, 'tis cheaper keeping a wife than a wench.

DAPPERWIT
If you are so melancholy, sir, we will have the fiddles and a dance to divert you; come!

[A Dance.

GRIPE
Indeed, you have put me so upon a merry pin, that I resolve to marry too.

LADY FLIPPANT
Nay, if my brother come to marrying once, I may too; I swore I would, when he did, little thinking—

SIR SIMON ADDLEPLOT
I take you at your word, madam.

LADY FLIPPANT
Well, but if I had thought you would have been so quick with me—

GRIPE
Where is your parson?

DAPPERWIT
What! you would not revenge yourself upon the parson?

GRIPE

No, I would have the parson revenge me upon you; he should marry me.

DAPPERWIT
I am glad you are so frolic, sir; but who would you marry?

GRIPE
That innocent lady.

[Pointing to **LUCY**.

DAPPERWIT
That innocent lady!

GRIPE
Nay, I am impatient, Mrs. Joyner; pray fetch him up if he be yet in the house.

DAPPERWIT
We were not married here:—but you cannot be in earnest.

GRIPE
You'll find it so; since you have robbed me of my housekeeper, I must get another.

DAPPERWIT
Why, she was my wench!

GRIPE
I'll make her honest then.

MRS CROSSBITE
Upon my repute he never saw her before:—but will your worship marry my daughter then?

GRIPE
I promise her and you, before all this good company, to-morrow I will make her my wife.

DAPPERWIT
How!

RANGER [To **VALENTINE**]
Our ladies, sir, I suppose, expect the same promise from us.

VALENTINE
They may be sure of us without a promise; but let us (if we can) obtain theirs, to be sure of them.

DAPPERWIT [To **GRIPE**]
But will you marry her to-morrow?—.

GRIPE
I will, verily.

DAPPERWIT
I am undone then! ruined, let me perish!

SIR SIMON ADDLEPLOT
No, you may hire a little room in Covent Garden, and set up a coffee-house:—you and your wife will be sure of the wits' custom.

DAPPERWIT
Abused by him I have abused!—
Fortune our foe we cannot overwit;
By none but thee our projects are cross-bit.

VALENTINE
Come, dear madam, what, yet angry?—jealousy sure is much more pardonable before marriage than after it; but to-morrow, by the help of the parson, you'll put me out of all my fears.

CHRISTINA
I am afraid then you would give me my revenge, and make me jealous of you; and I had rather suspect your faith than you should mine.

RANGER
Cousin Lydia, I had rather suspect your faith too, than you should mine; therefore let us e'en marry to-morrow, that I may have my turn of watching, dogging, standing under the window, at the door, behind the hanging, or—

LYDIA
But if I could be desperate now and give you up my liberty, could you find in your heart to quit all other engagements, and voluntarily turn yourself over to one woman, and she a wife too? could you away with the insupportable bondage of matrimony?

RANGER
You talk of matrimony as irreverently as my Lady Flippant: the bondage of matrimony! no—
The end of marriage now is liberty.
And two are bound—to set each other free.

EPILOGUE

SPOKEN BY **DAPPERWIT**.

Now my brisk brothers of the pit, you'll say
I'm come to speak a good word for the play;
But gallants, let me perish! if I do,
For I have wit and judgment, just like you;
Wit never partial, judgment free and bold,
For fear or friendship never bought or sold,

Nor by good-nature e'er to be cajoled.
Good-nature in a critic were a crime,
Like mercy in a judge, and renders him
Guilty of all those faults he does forgive,
Besides, if thief from gallows you reprieve,
He'll cut your throat; so poet saved from shame,
In damned lampoon will murder your good name.
Yet in true spite to him and to his play,
Good faith, you should not rail at them to-day
But to be more his foe, seem most his friend,
And so maliciously the play commend;
That he may be betrayed to writing on,
And poet let him be,—to be undone.

www.ingramcontent.com/pod-product-compliance
Lightning Source LLC
Chambersburg PA
CBHW022117040426
42450CB00006B/739